Mathematics for Christian Living Series

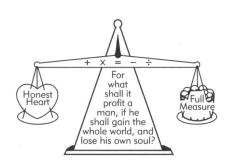

Honest Heart

Full Measure

For what shall it profit a man, if he shall gain the whole world, and lose his own soul?

Mathematics for Christian Living Series

Working Arithmetic

Grade 2

Unit 5, Lessons 138–170

Rod and Staff Publishers, Inc.

P.O. Box 3, Hwy. 172

Crockett, Kentucky 41413

Telephone: (606) 522-4348

Acknowledgments

We are indebted to God for the vision of the need for a *Mathematics for Christian Living Series* and for His enabling grace. Charitable contributions from many churches have helped to cover the expenses for research and development.

This revision was written by Sisters Miriam Rudolph and Marla Martin. The brethren Marvin Eicher, Jerry Kreider, and Luke Sensenig served as editors. Most of the illustrations were drawn by Lois Myer. The work was evaluated by a panel of reviewers and tested by teachers in the classroom. Much effort was devoted to the production of the book. We are grateful for all who helped to make this book possible.

—The Publishers

This book is part of a course for grade 2 arithmetic and will be most effective if used with the other parts of the course. *Working Arithmetic* includes the following items:

Teacher's Manual, part 1 (Units 1, 2)
Teacher's Manual, part 2 (Units 3–5)
Pupil's Workbook, Unit 1
Pupil's Workbook, Unit 2
Pupil's Workbook, Unit 3
Pupil's Workbook, Unit 4
Pupil's Workbook, Unit 5
Blacklines

Copyright 1992

by

Rod and Staff Publishers, Inc.
Crockett, Kentucky 41413

Printed in U.S.A.

ISBN 978-07399-0458-9

Catalog no. 13225.3

16   17   18   —   24   23   22   21   20   19

Unit 5 Contents

This list shows what concepts are introduced in these lessons. Each concept is also reviewed in following lessons.

138. (16) 9 7 triplet and facts
     Half dollar + pennies
139.
140.
141. Fraction: $\frac{1}{3}$
142.
143.
144.
145.
146. (16) 8 8 triplet and facts
147.
148.
149. (17) 9 8 triplet and facts
     Equation: 2 cups = 1 pint

150.
151. Equation: 2 pints = 1 quart
152.
153.
154.
155. Equation: 4 quarts = 1 gallon
156.
157. (18) 9 9 triplet and facts
158. Equation: 16 ounces = 1 pound
159.
160–170. Review

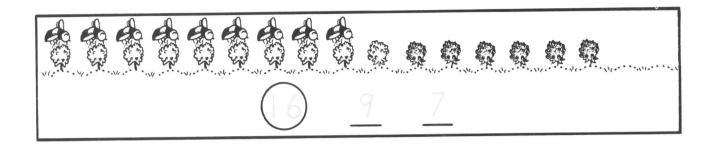

16   9   7

"Jonathan . . . said, I did but taste a little honey." 1 Samuel 14:43

16 −9	16 −7	16 −9	9 +7	7 +9	16 −7	16 −9	9 +7
16 −7	16 −9	9 +7	16 −7	16 −9	7 +9	16 −7	9 +7
16 −7	16 −9	7 +9	16 −9	16 −7	9 +7	7 +9	16 −9
16 −9	16 −7	16 −7	7 +9	9 +7	16 −9	7 +9	16 −7
16 −9	16 −7	16 −9	16 −9	7 +9	16 −7	16 −9	7 +9

16 −7	9 +7	16 −9	16 −9	16 −7	16 −9

138

```
  578        328        247        486        157        458
 +267       +596       +128       +369       +608       +184
_____     _____     _____     _____     _____     _____
```

```
  463        475        246        357        157        138
 +288       +169       +248       +394       +488       +356
_____     _____     _____     _____     _____     _____
```

```
  259        228        579        127        266        459
 +383       +537       +276       +248       +658       +386
_____     _____     _____     _____     _____     _____
```

 _____

 _____

 _____

Speed
Drill

15	8	9	15	8	15
−6	+7	+6	−7	+7	−9

15	15	7	15	6	8
−8	−6	+8	−9	+9	+7

15	15	15	6	15	9	8	15
−8	−6	−9	+9	−7	+6	+7	−6

15	15	6	7	15	8	15	15
−6	−8	+9	+8	−9	+7	−6	−8

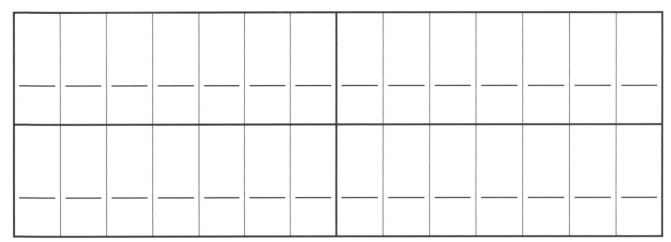

"Whatsoever thy hand findeth to do, do it with thy might." Ecclesiastes 9:10

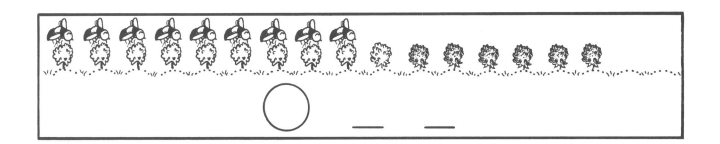

○ ___ ___

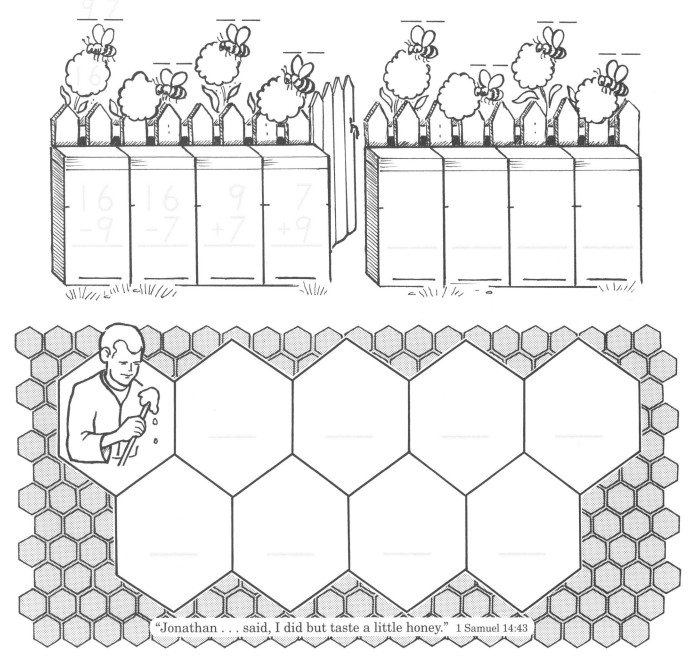

9 7
___ ___   ___ ___

16
___

| 16 | 16 | 9 | 7 |
| -9 | -7 | +7 | +9 |

"Jonathan . . . said, I did but taste a little honey." 1 Samuel 14:43

16 −7	16 −9	16 −7	9 +7	7 +9	16 −7	16 −9	9 +7
16 −7	16 −9	7 +9	16 −7	16 −9	7 +9	16 −7	16 −9
16 −9	16 −7	9 +7	16 −7	16 −7	9 +7	7 +9	16 −9
16 −9	16 −7	16 −7	7 +9	9 +7	16 −9	16 −9	16 −7
16 −9	16 −7	16 −9	16 −9	7 +9	16 −7	16 −9	7 +9

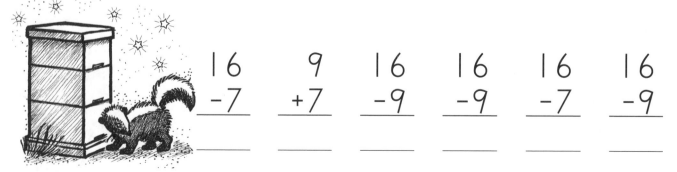

16 −7	9 +7	16 −9	16 −9	16 −7	16 −9

85 -28	56 +87	84 -56	84 -35	67 +78	85 -38
68 +85	95 -49	46 +79	74 -28	76 +77	87 +38
76 +67	94 -37	95 -46	95 -67	73 -26	76 +69

_____

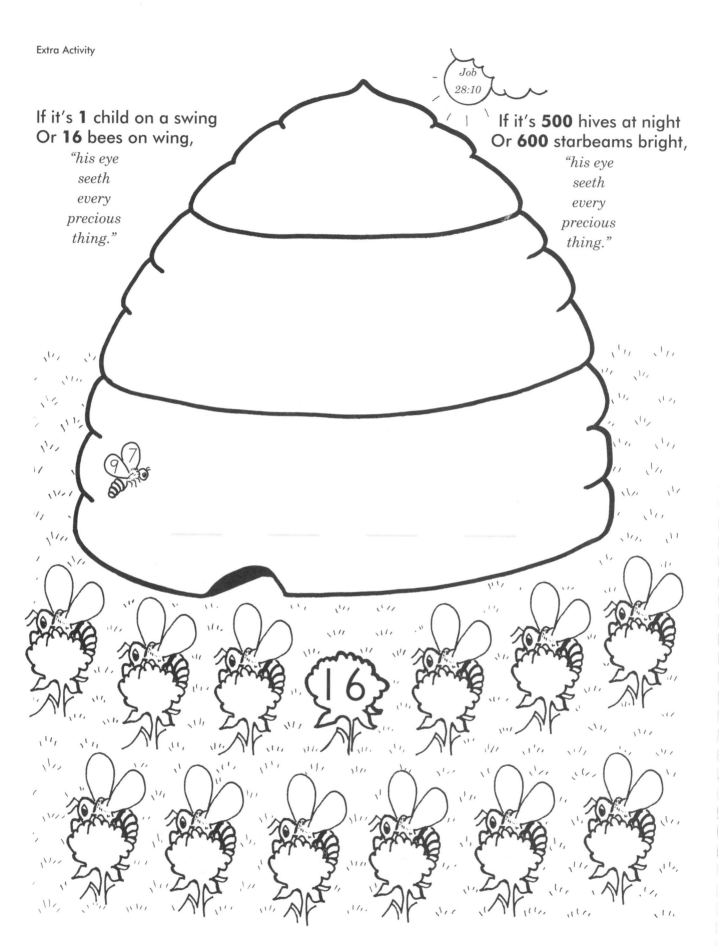

If it's **1** child on a swing
Or **16** bees on wing,
"his eye
seeth
every
precious
thing."

Job
28:10

If it's **500** hives at night
Or **600** starbeams bright,
"his eye
seeth
every
precious
thing."

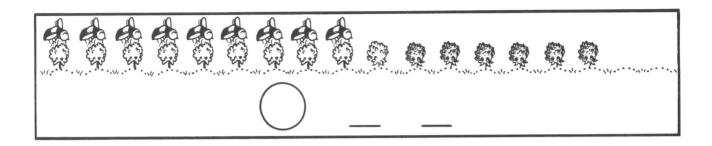

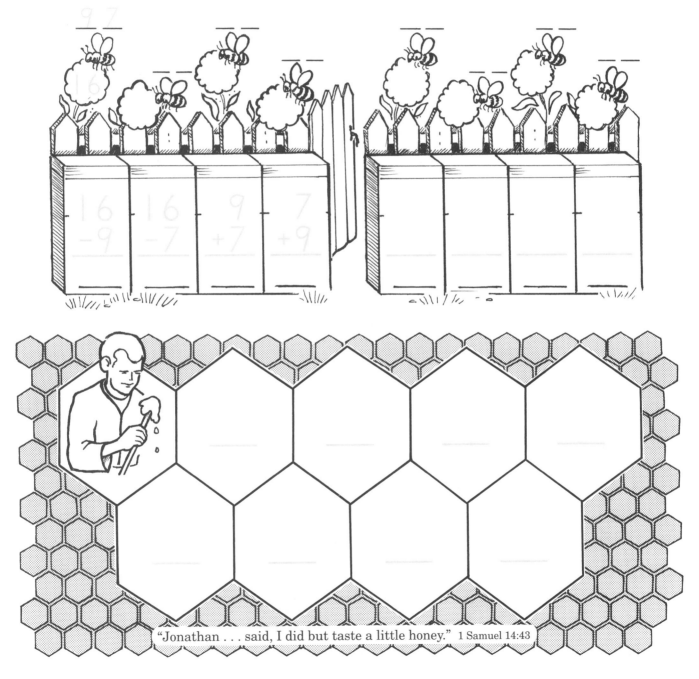

"Jonathan . . . said, I did but taste a little honey." 1 Samuel 14:43

15

168	58	169	168	73	169
-97	+77	-74	-96	+86	-76

76	169	68	166	72	167
+79	-72	+77	-94	+86	-94

78	169	168	76	167	57
+77	-77	-94	+83	-75	+38

168	83	168	87	167	67
-95	+75	-96	+58	-70	+88

166	84	167	167	77	169
-73	+75	-95	-72	+58	-98

75	169	167	67
+84	-95	-75	+88

Lee has 37¢ in his
bank. Grandfather gives
him 58¢ for his birthday.
How many cents does
Lee have now?

Fifteen children play
tag. Eight children are
on base. How many
children are not on
base?

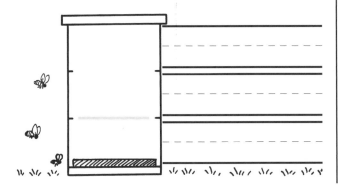

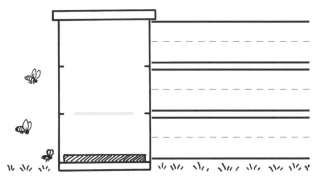

Speed
Drill

15	9	16	15	8	7
-7	+7	-7	-8	+7	+9

16	15	7	7	16	9
-9	-8	+9	+8	-7	+7

15	15	9	8	16	16	9	15
-8	-7	+7	+7	-9	-7	+7	-7

15	16	7	16	7	9	15	16
-7	-9	+9	-7	+8	+7	-8	-9

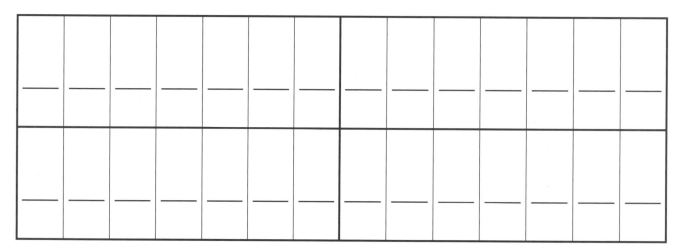

"Whatsoever thy hand findeth to do, do it with thy might." Ecclesiastes 9:10

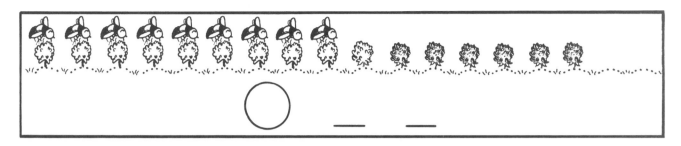

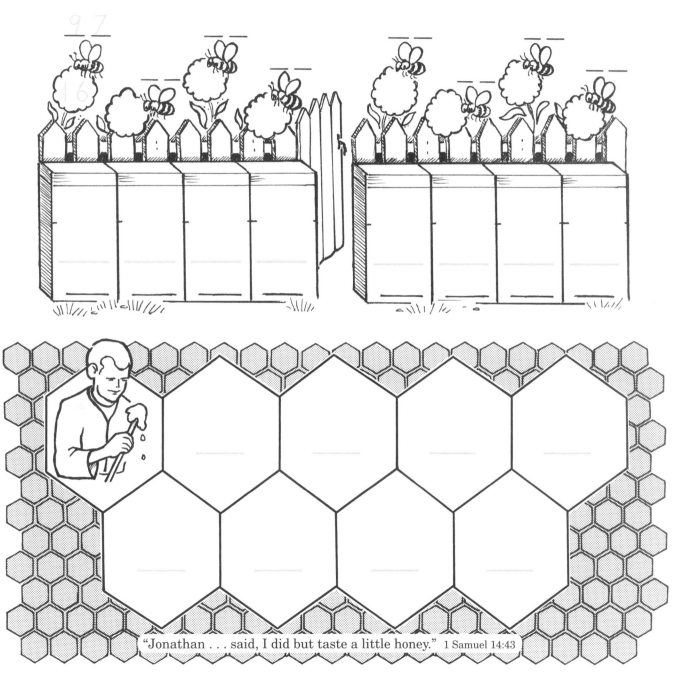

"Jonathan . . . said, I did but taste a little honey." 1 Samuel 14:43

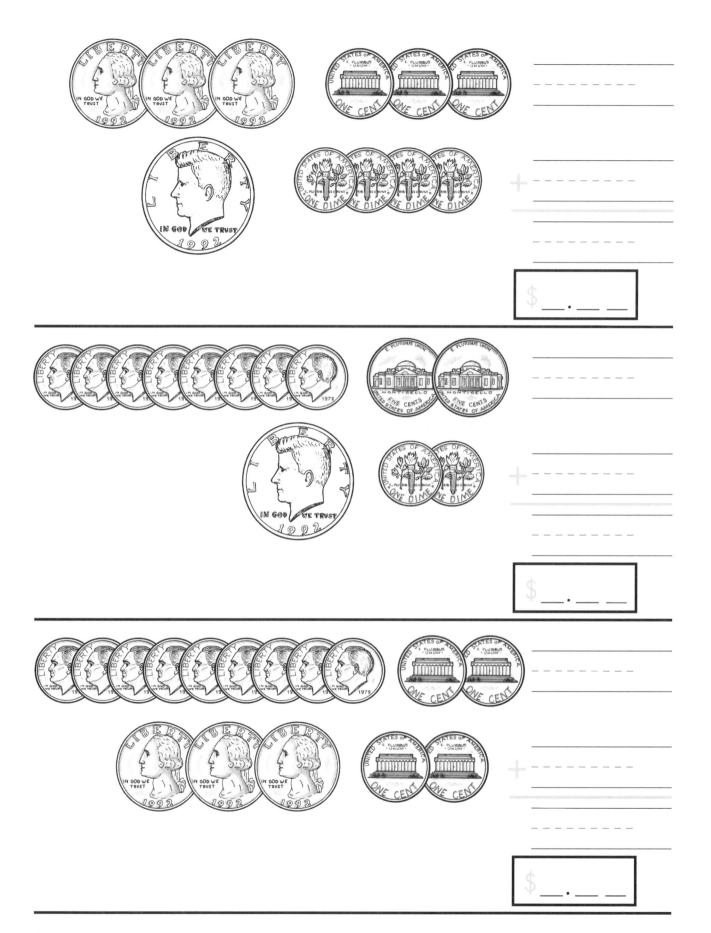

96 −79	99 −76	95 −37	96 −67	77 −47	96 −57
75 −28	99 −70	96 −39	75 −47	95 −28	66 −39
65 −26	84 −26	57 −34	95 −65	66 −37	55 −38

Write $\frac{1}{3}$ on each **third**.

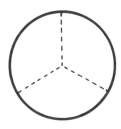
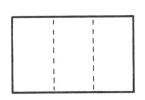

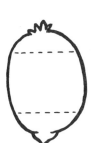
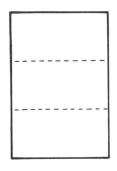

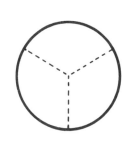
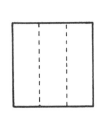

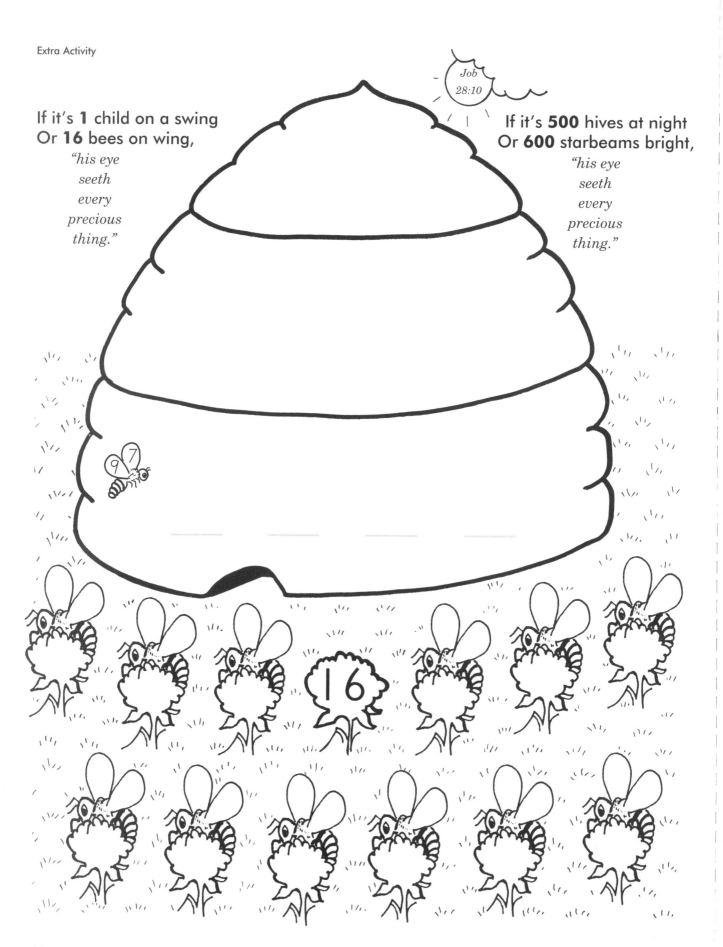

If it's **1** child on a swing
Or **16** bees on wing,

"his eye
seeth
every
precious
thing."

Job 28:10

If it's **500** hives at night
Or **600** starbeams bright,

"his eye
seeth
every
precious
thing."

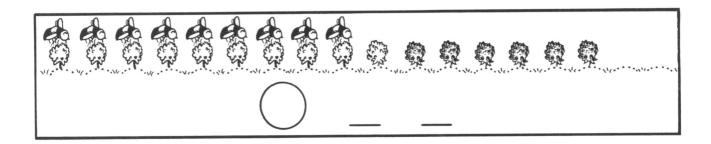

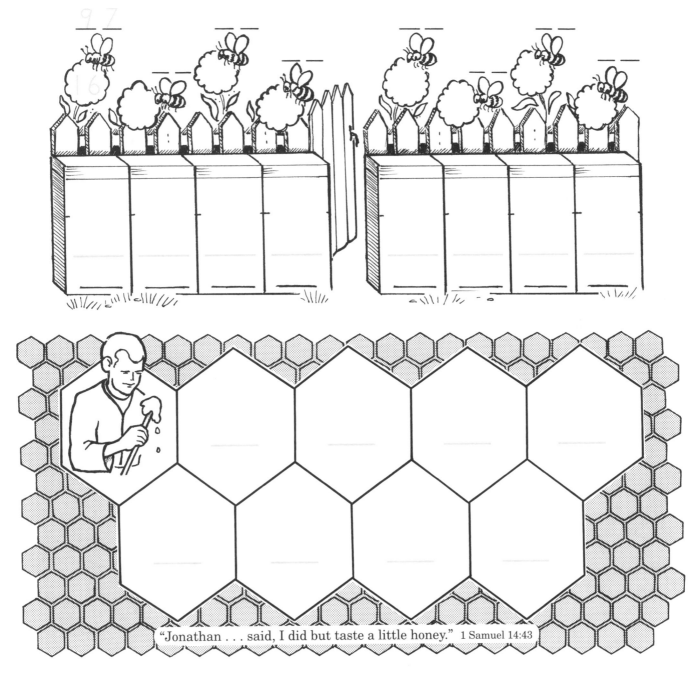

"Jonathan . . . said, I did but taste a little honey." 1 Samuel 14:43

$9 + \underline{} = 16$	$16 - \underline{} = 7$	$\underline{} - 7 = 9$
$7 + \underline{} = 16$	$\underline{} + 9 = 16$	$7 + \underline{} = 16$
$16 - \underline{} = 7$	$\underline{} - 9 = 7$	$16 - 9 = \underline{}$
$16 - \underline{} = 9$	$16 - 7 = \underline{}$	$\underline{} - 7 = 9$
$\underline{} + 9 = 16$	$7 + \underline{} = 16$	$7 + \underline{} = 16$
$\underline{} - 9 = 7$	$9 + 7 = \underline{}$	$\underline{} - 9 = 7$

$$
\begin{array}{cccccccc}
5 & 4 & 2 & 4 & 5 & 1 & 1 & 2 \\
4 & 3 & 7 & 2 & 3 & 8 & 6 & 5 \\
+7 & +9 & +7 & +7 & +7 & +7 & +9 & +9 \\
\hline
\end{array}
$$

$$
\begin{array}{cccccccc}
6 & 7 & 6 & 4 & 3 & 5 & 7 & 4 \\
3 & 2 & 3 & 5 & 4 & 2 & 2 & 4 \\
+6 & +5 & +7 & +7 & +9 & +9 & +2 & +6 \\
\hline
\end{array}
$$

9	16	15	6	16	9	14	16
+7	−7	−9	+9	−9	+6	−5	−7

15	9	15	8	16	7	7	15
−8	+7	−7	+7	−9	+9	+8	−7

16	15	6	16	7	15	15	7
−7	−6	+9	−9	+8	−9	−6	+9

Write $\frac{1}{3}$ on each **third**.

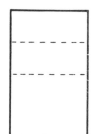
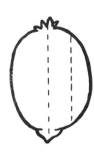

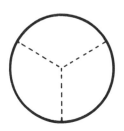

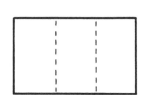

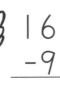

Speed Drill

15	16	15	9	16	9
-6	-9	-9	+7	-7	+6

16	15	6	7	15	16
-9	-9	+9	+9	-6	-7

16	7	9	15	9	15	16	16
-7	+9	+6	-6	+7	-9	-9	-7

9	16	15	16	7	6	15	16
+7	-7	-6	-7	+9	+9	-9	-9

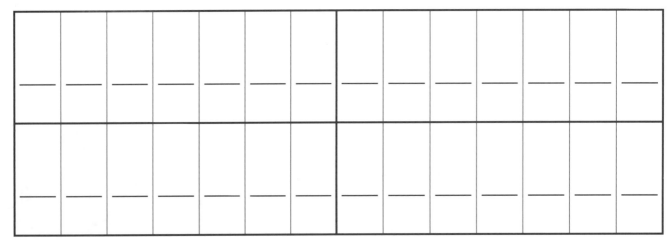

"Whatsoever thy hand findeth to do, do it with thy might." Ecclesiastes 9:10

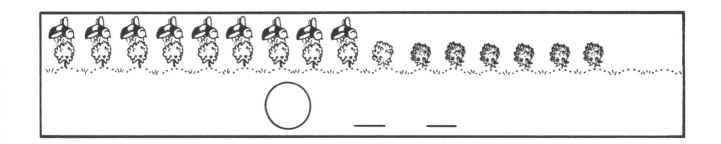

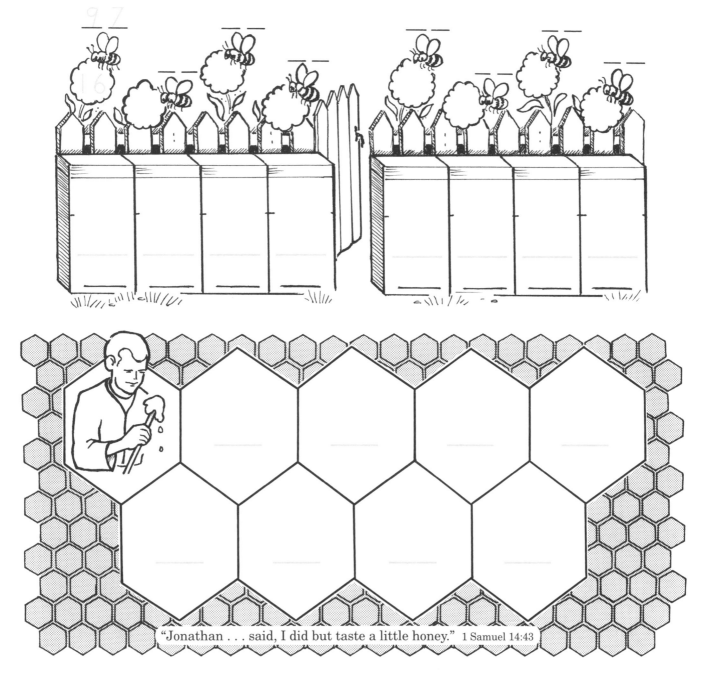

"Jonathan . . . said, I did but taste a little honey." 1 Samuel 14:43

God made the sun to shine. Soon 16 buds opened. 7 buds were yellow. The rest were red. How many buds were red?

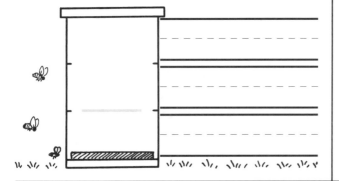

Father has one dozen stamps in his desk. He sticks 5 stamps on letters. How many stamps are left in his desk?

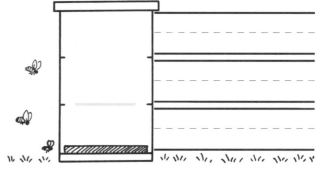

Mother pays 27¢ for a box of salt and 69¢ for a bag of nuts. How many cents does she pay for both things?

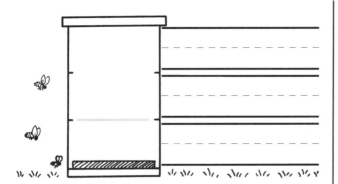

A skunk scratched on a hive. 16 bees flew out. The skunk ate 9 of them. How many bees did the skunk not eat?

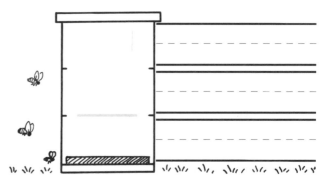

```
  66      57      86      85      66      65
 -59     +88     -57     -37     +79     -28
_____   _____   _____   _____   _____   _____


  89      66      67      95      76      57
 +67     -47     +99     -76     +79     +99
_____   _____   _____   _____   _____   _____


  95      94      95      96      86      76
 -58     -37     -47     -67     -29     -69
_____   _____   _____   _____   _____   _____
```

Write $\frac{1}{3}$ on each **third**.

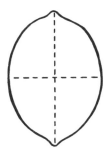
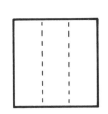
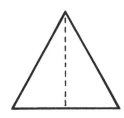

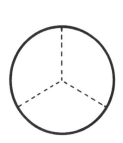
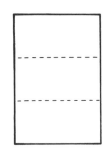
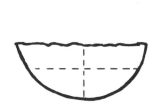
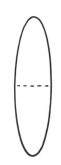
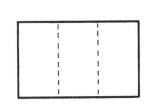

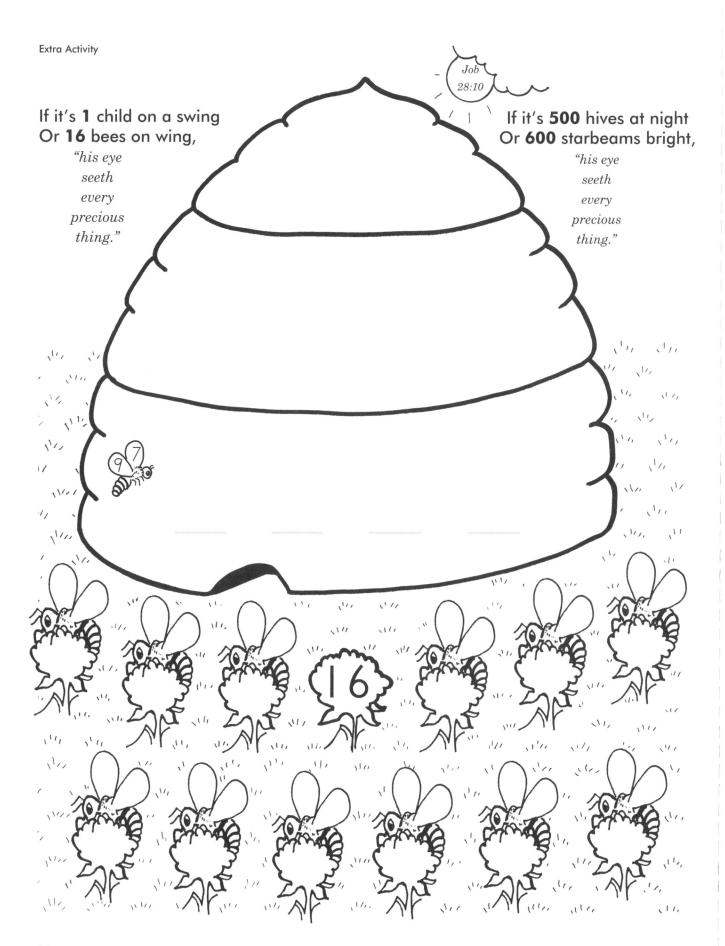

If it's **1** child on a swing
Or **16** bees on wing,
"his eye
seeth
every
precious
thing."

Job 28:10

If it's **500** hives at night
Or **600** starbeams bright,
"his eye
seeth
every
precious
thing."

30

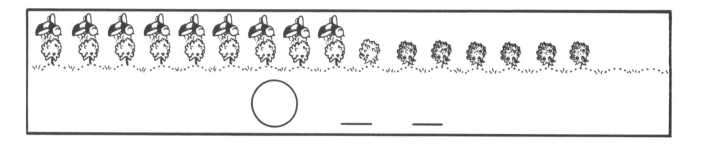

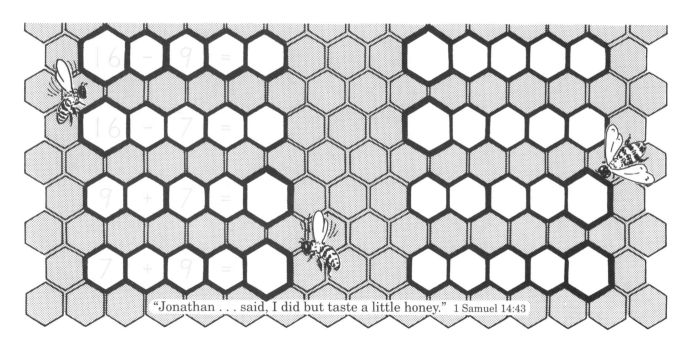

"Jonathan . . . said, I did but taste a little honey." 1 Samuel 14:43

16	16	15	16	9	15	15	7
-9	-7	-9	-7	+7	-9	-6	+9

9	16	9	7	15	6	15	16
+7	-7	+6	+9	-6	+9	-6	-9

16	16	7	16	6	9	16	9
-7	-9	+9	-9	+9	+7	-9	+6

6	9	15	9	16	15	7	15
+9	+7	-9	+6	-9	-9	+9	-6

16	6	15	16	9	15	16	15
-7	+9	-9	-9	+7	-6	-9	-9

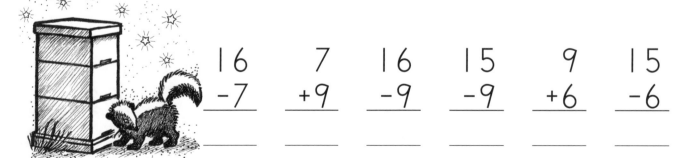

16	7	16	15	9	15
-7	+9	-9	-9	+6	-6

```
  74      52      56      24      43      45
  15      37      12      44      34      32
 +67     +76     +66     +97     +69     +79
_____   _____   _____   _____   _____   _____
```

```
  35      44      61      35      54      34
  43      23      95      63      43      93
 + 5     + 9     + 8     + 7     + 7     + 9
_____   _____   _____   _____   _____   _____
```

Write $\frac{1}{3}$ on each **third**.

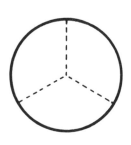

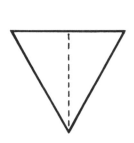

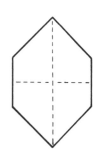

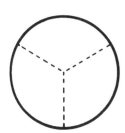

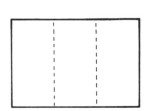

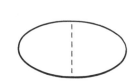

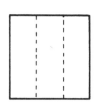

Speed
Drill

7	16	15	8	15	7
+9	-7	-6	+7	-7	+9

7	15	16	16	15	15
+8	-9	-9	-7	-8	-6

9	16	7	15	8	15	16	9
+7	-7	+9	-7	+7	-6	-7	+7

15	7	16	15	15	16	15	7
-6	+9	-7	-8	-6	-9	-9	+8

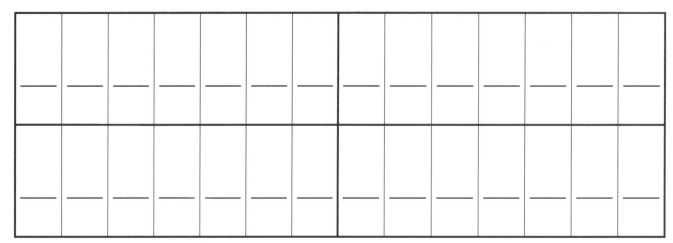

"Whatsoever thy hand findeth to do, do it with thy might."   Ecclesiastes 9:10

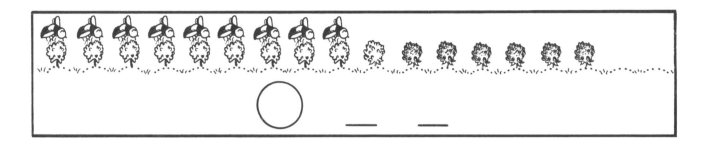

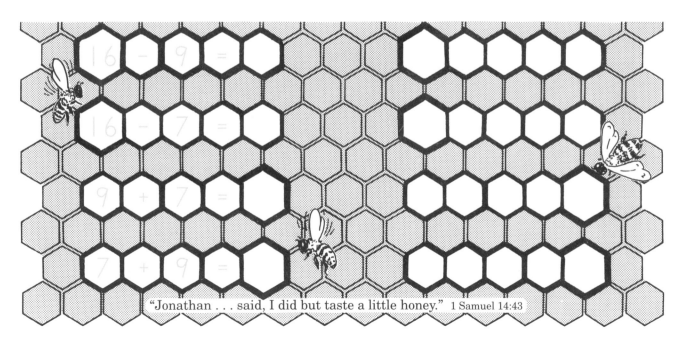

"Jonathan . . . said, I did but taste a little honey." 1 Samuel 14:43

16	13	14	9	9	13	15	8
-9	-4	-8	+7	+6	-8	-9	+6

14	15	5	15	13	6	13	8
-7	-7	+8	-6	-5	+9	-9	+5

16	15	7	15	14	8	7	13
-7	-8	+9	-9	-9	+7	+7	-7

14	13	14	6	7	14	7	13
-6	-6	-5	+7	+8	-6	+6	-9

16	6	15	7	9	16	16	9
-9	+8	-8	+9	+4	-7	-9	+5

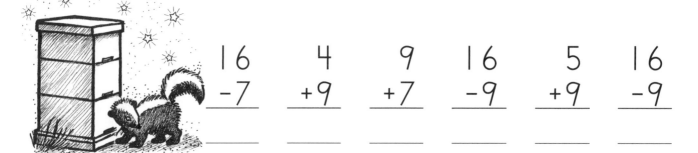

16	4	9	16	5	16
-7	+9	+7	-9	+9	-9

| 279 | 537 | 266 | 446 | 355 | 289 |
| +367 | +268 | +529 | +338 | +449 | +467 |

| 487 | 526 | 349 | 259 | 149 | 118 |
| +269 | +359 | +355 | +497 | +736 | +586 |

| 468 | 467 | 555 | 359 | 457 | 126 |
| +337 | +179 | +229 | +436 | +299 | +678 |

Write $\frac{1}{2}$ on each **half**.

Write $\frac{1}{4}$ on each **fourth**.

Write $\frac{1}{3}$ on each **third**.

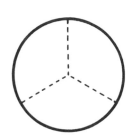
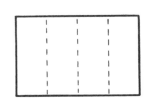
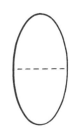

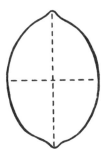
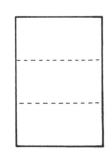
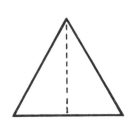
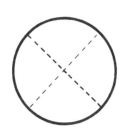
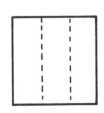

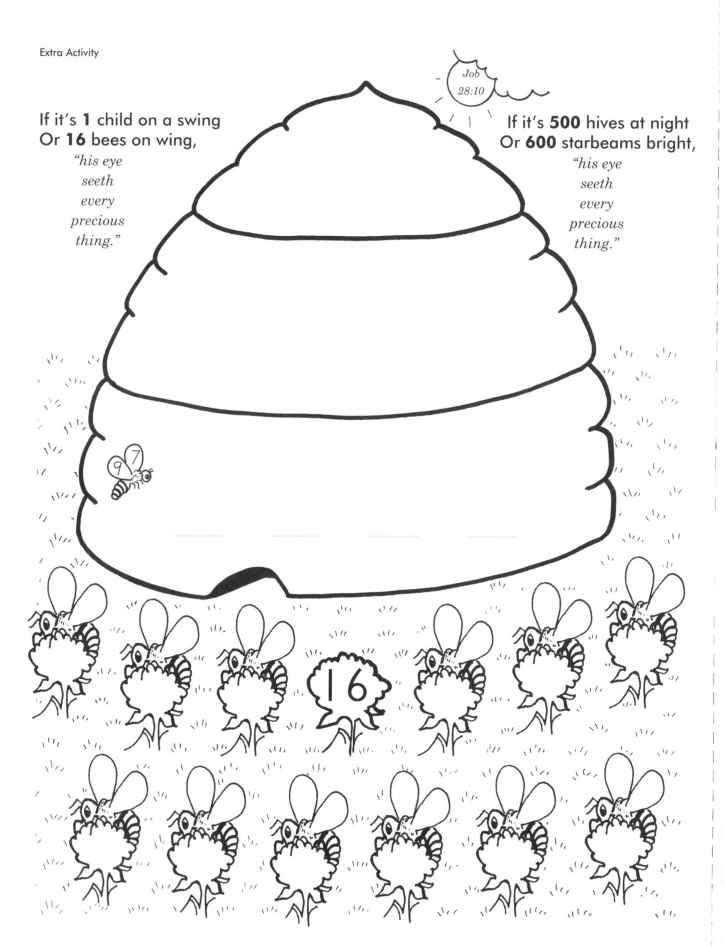

If it's **1** child on a swing
Or **16** bees on wing,

*"his eye
seeth
every
precious
thing."*

*Job
28:10*

If it's **500** hives at night
Or **600** starbeams bright,

*"his eye
seeth
every
precious
thing."*

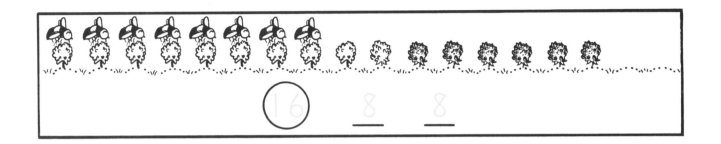

(16)   _8_   _8_

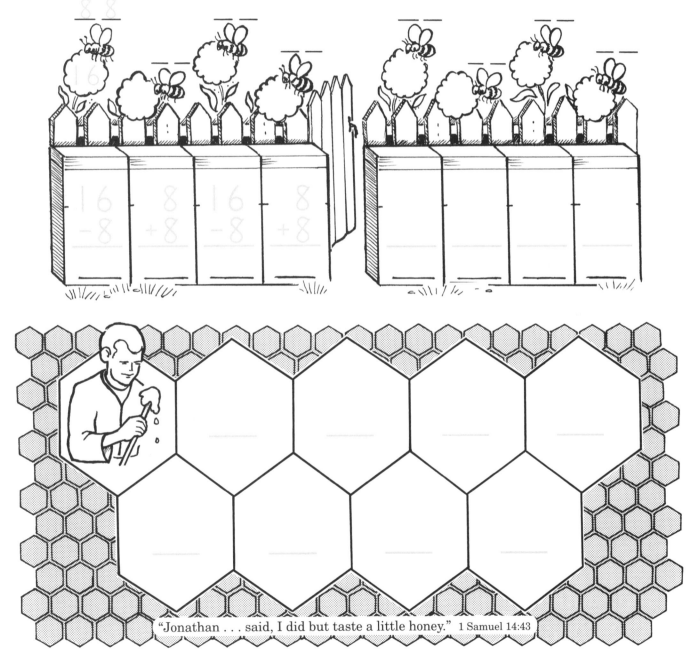

16   8   16   8
-8   +8   -8   +8

"Jonathan . . . said, I did but taste a little honey."   1 Samuel 14:43

16	15	15	16	8	15	15	8
−8	−8	−7	−8	+8	−7	−8	+7

7	15	8	8	16	8	15	16
+8	−8	+8	+8	−8	+8	−8	−8

15	16	8	16	8	7	15	7
−7	−8	+7	−8	+7	+8	−7	+8

8	8	15	7	16	15	8	16
+7	+8	−8	+8	−8	−8	+8	−8

15	16	15	16	8	15	16	7
−8	−8	−7	−8	+8	−7	−8	+8

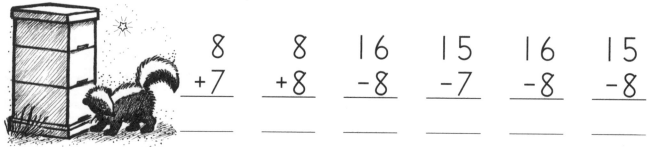

8	8	16	15	16	15
+7	+8	−8	−7	−8	−8

40

86 −48	78 +78	95 −88	86 −58	67 +89	75 −48
88 +58	96 −38	96 −29	85 −27	57 +89	95 −19
66 −39	76 +89	96 −68	54 −47	87 +78	66 −28

Write $\frac{1}{2}$ on each **half**.

Write $\frac{1}{4}$ on each **fourth**.

Write $\frac{1}{3}$ on each **third**.

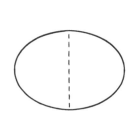
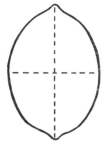
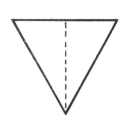

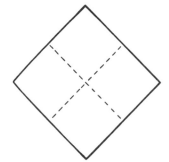
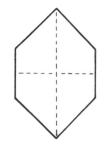
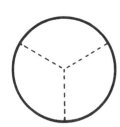
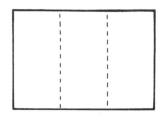

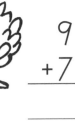

Speed
Drill

16	15	6	15	9	14
-7	-9	+9	-6	+7	-9

9	5	16	9	7	14
+7	+9	-9	+6	+9	-5

16	16	14	7	16	6	15	15
-7	-9	-9	+9	-7	+9	-9	-6

16	15	16	9	9	16	9	7
-9	-6	-7	+7	+6	-9	+5	+9

"Whatsoever thy hand findeth to do, do it with thy might." Ecclesiastes 9:10

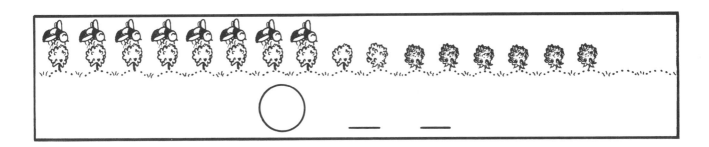

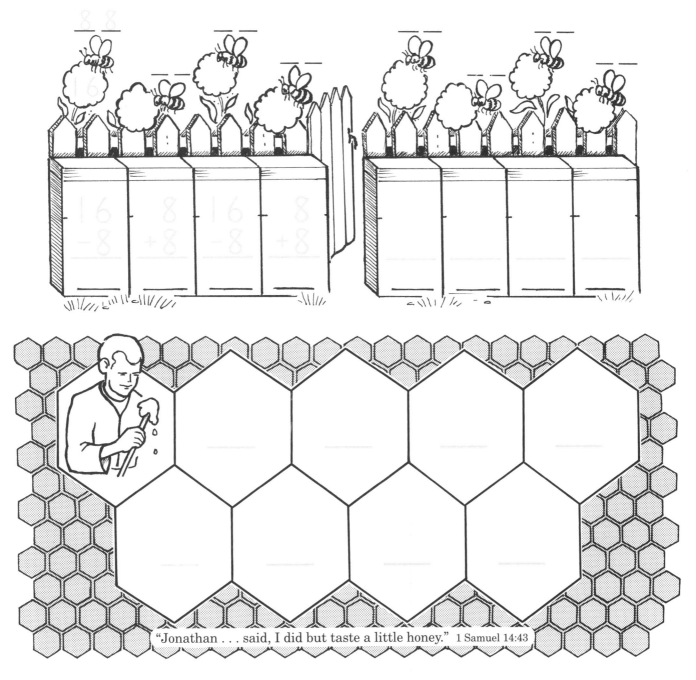

"Jonathan . . . said, I did but taste a little honey." 1 Samuel 14:43

169	78	169	157	73	166
−87	+87	−84	−85	+86	−86

78	169	83	156	72	167
+78	−82	+85	−74	+86	−84

78	169	158	86	167	58
+78	−87	−84	+83	−85	+38

168	83	158	84	167	68
−85	+75	−76	+84	−80	+88

164	84	158	167	77	166
−84	+75	−86	−82	+88	−84

85	159	167	68
+84	−85	−85	+88

147

 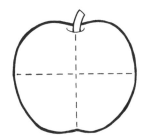

Write $\frac{1}{2}$ on each **half**.

Write $\frac{1}{4}$ on each **fourth**.

Write $\frac{1}{3}$ on each **third**.

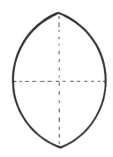 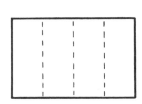 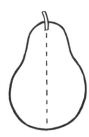

 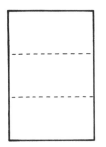 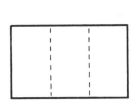 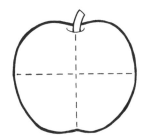 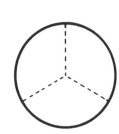

45

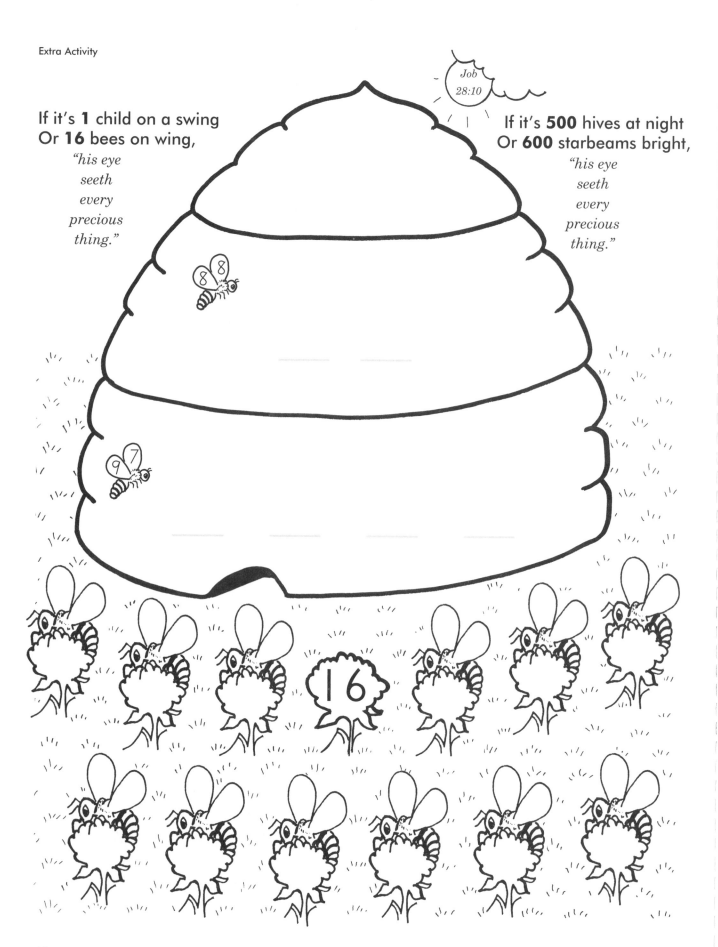

If it's **1** child on a swing
Or **16** bees on wing,

*"his eye
seeth
every
precious
thing."*

*Job
28:10*

If it's **500** hives at night
Or **600** starbeams bright,

*"his eye
seeth
every
precious
thing."*

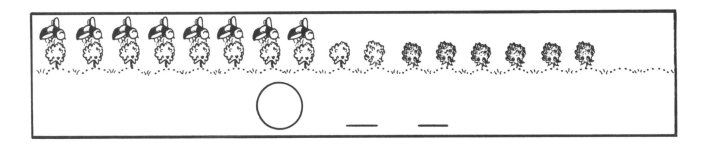

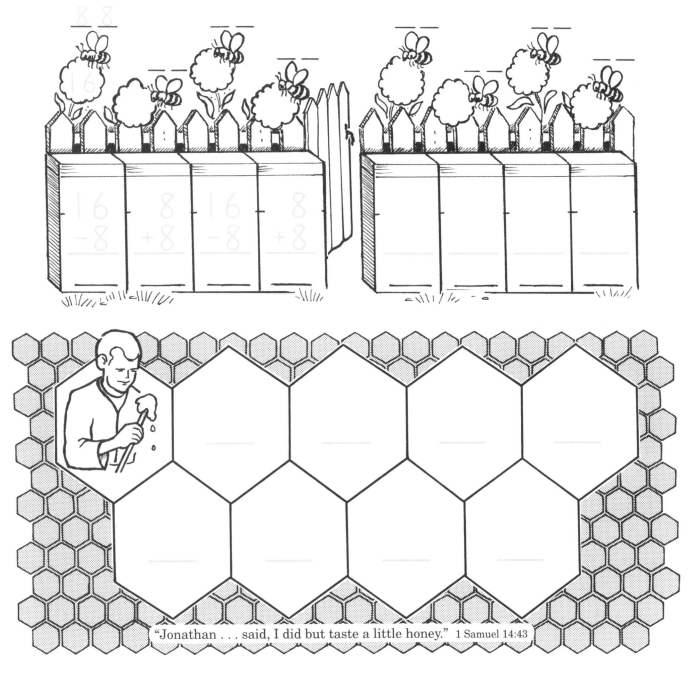

"Jonathan . . . said, I did but taste a little honey."   1 Samuel 14:43

47

Father has 83 tulips in his greenhouse and 85 tulips in his yard. How many tulips in all does Father have?

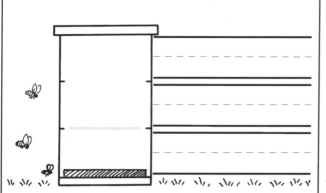

Sixteen robins sail in the sky. Then 7 robins fly down to their nests. How many robins are still in the sky?

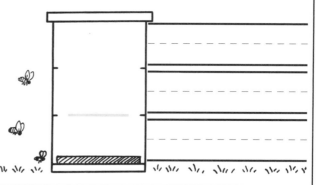

6	3	4	4	5	2	3	4
2	5	4	2	3	7	6	4
+8	+8	+8	+8	+8	+6	+7	+6

7	2	6	1	4	7	8	6
2	6	3	7	5	1	0	3
+5	+8	+6	+8	+5	+8	+8	+7

578	378	486	488	705	458
+268	+586	+309	+358	+208	+346

547	335	458	607	275	567
+248	+578	+388	+197	+689	+279

8	16	6	9	15	5	15	15
+8	-8	+9	+7	-8	+9	-9	-6

16	14	6	16	8	7	15	7
-7	-8	+8	-9	+8	+8	-7	+9

9	7	16	7	15	16	8	15
+7	+8	-8	+9	-7	-9	+7	-8

148

15	16	8	15	7	8
-7	-8	+8	-8	+8	+8

15	15	8	8	15	7
-8	-7	+8	+7	-7	+8

8	15	8	7	15	8	16	15
+8	-7	+8	+8	-8	+8	-8	-7

16	8	8	16	7	8	16	15
-8	+8	+7	-8	+8	+8	-8	-8

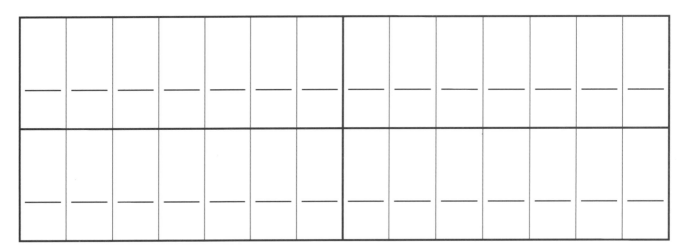

"Whatsoever thy hand findeth to do, do it with thy might." Ecclesiastes 9:10

50

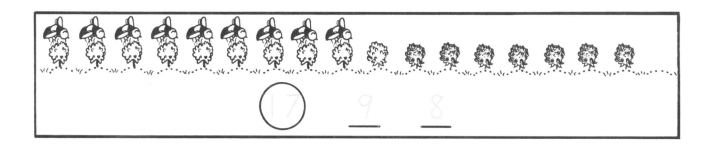

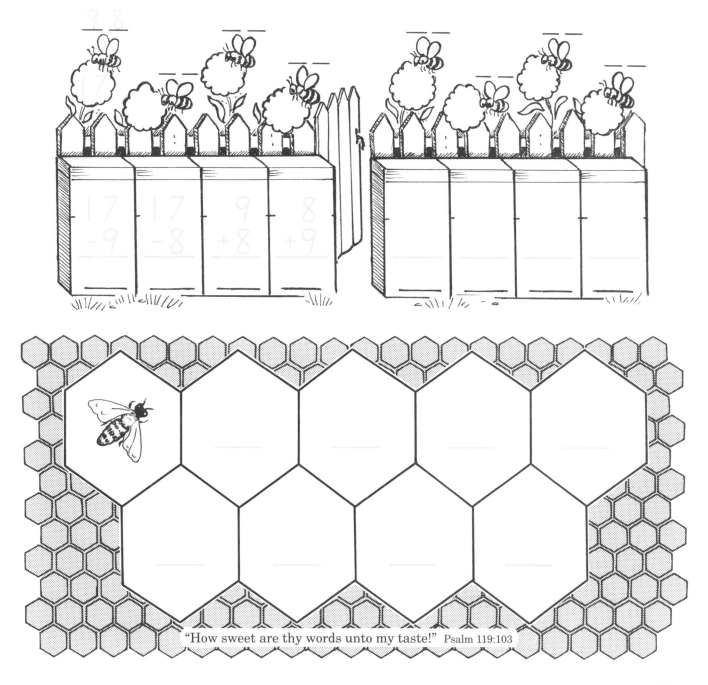

"How sweet are thy words unto my taste!" Psalm 119:103

17	9	17	17	9	17
-9	+8	-8	-9	+8	-9

8	9	17	8	17	17	8	17
+9	+8	-9	+9	-9	-8	+9	-9

17	9	17	8	9	8	17	17
-8	+8	-9	+9	+8	+9	-8	-9

8	17	17	8	17	17	8	17
+9	-8	-9	+9	-8	-9	+9	-8

9	17	8	17	9	9	17	17
+8	-8	+9	-9	+8	+8	-9	-8

17	9	9	17	17	17	17	9
-8	+8	+8	-9	-9	-8	-8	+8

```
  56        55        38        56        34        28
-  8      -  8      -  2        -7        -7        -4
_____    _____    _____    _____    _____    _____


  94        96        76        98        83        85
-56       -28       -69       -28       -15       -47
_____    _____    _____    _____    _____    _____


  75        83        95        79        86        65
-39       -56       -47       -55       -39       -16
_____    _____    _____    _____    _____    _____
```

2 cups   =   1 pint

If it's **1** child on a swing
Or **17** bees on wing,
*"his eye
seeth
every
precious
thing."*

*Job
28:10*

If it's **700** toads in spring
Or **800** birds that sing,
*"his eye
seeth
every
precious
thing."*

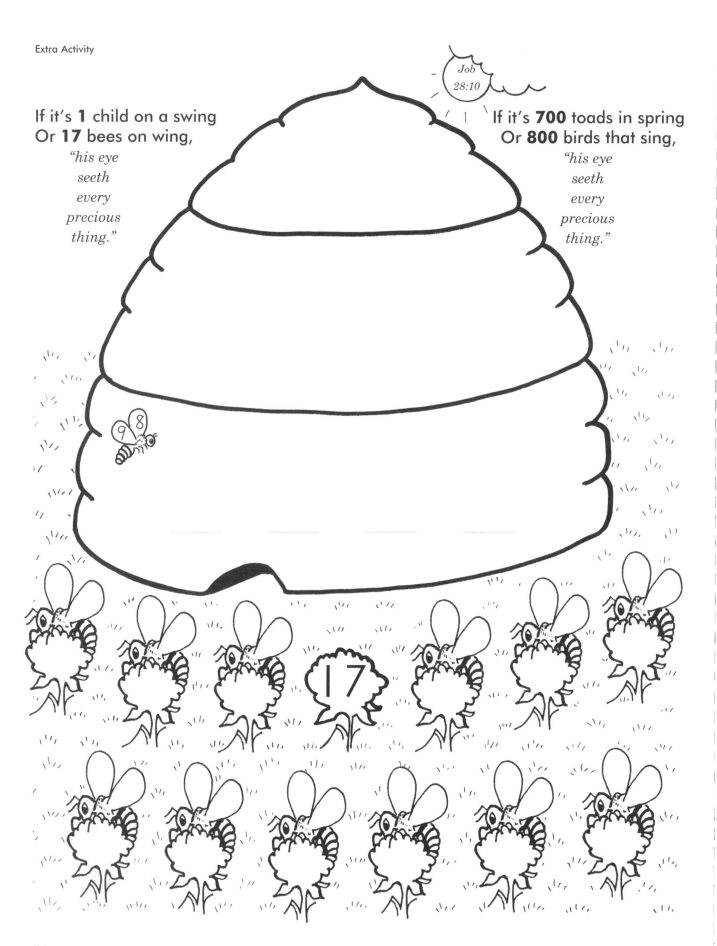

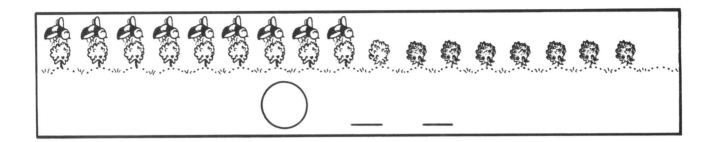

150

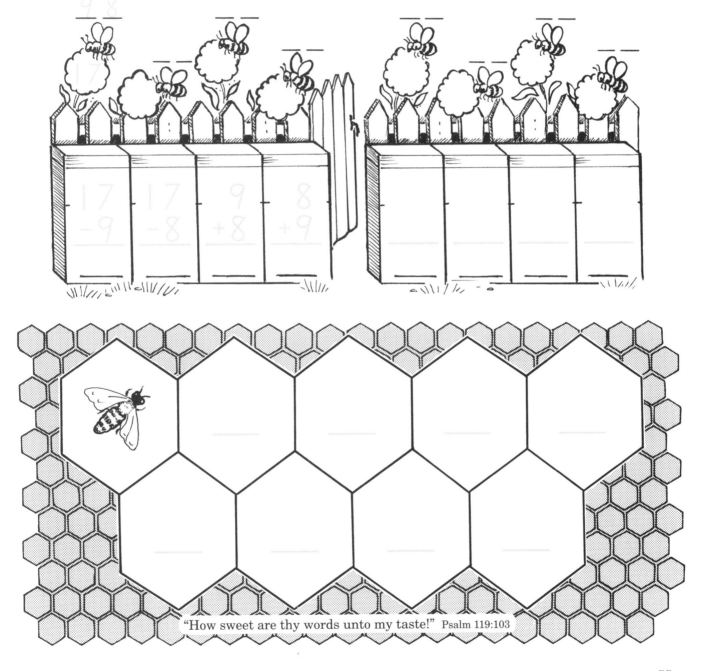

"How sweet are thy words unto my taste!" Psalm 119:103

	17	8	17	8	17	9
	-9	+9	-9	+9	-8	+8

17	17	8	17	9	17	9	17
-8	-8	+9	-8	+8	-9	+8	-9

8	17	17	17	8	17	17	17
+9	-8	-9	-9	+9	-9	-8	-8

17	8	17	9	17	17	9	9
-8	+9	-8	+8	-9	-8	+8	+8

17	17	17	8	17	17	17	9
-9	-8	-9	+9	-8	-9	-8	+8

8	9	17	17	8	17	8	17
+9	+8	-9	-8	+9	-9	+9	-9

```
  34        44        25        53        35        61
  23        34        43        32        22        25
 +79       +48       +37       +69       +28       +78
_____    _____    _____    _____    _____    _____


  32        45        33        54        40        36
  43        22        55        12        25        53
 +68       +33       +28       +95       +78       +45
_____    _____    _____    _____    _____    _____


  24        35        45        63        21        23
  53        23        12        22        48        34
 +28       +27       +79       +79       +57       +97
_____    _____    _____    _____    _____    _____
```

2 cups = 1 pint

9	17	8	17	17	17
+8	-9	+9	-8	-8	-9

17	9	8	17	9	17
-9	+8	+9	-8	+8	-8

17	9	17	17	17	8	17	9
-9	+8	-9	-8	-8	+9	-9	+8

8	17	17	8	17	9	8	17
+9	-9	-8	+9	-8	+8	+9	-9

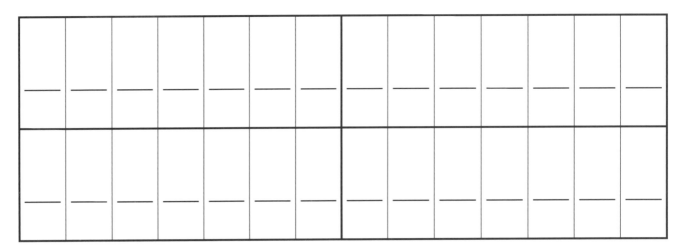

"Whatsoever thy hand findeth to do, do it with thy might." Ecclesiastes 9:10

58

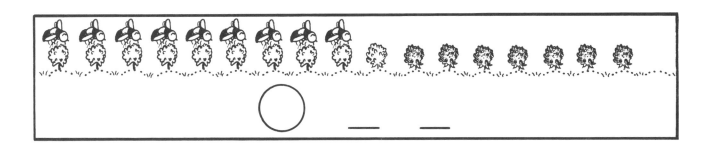

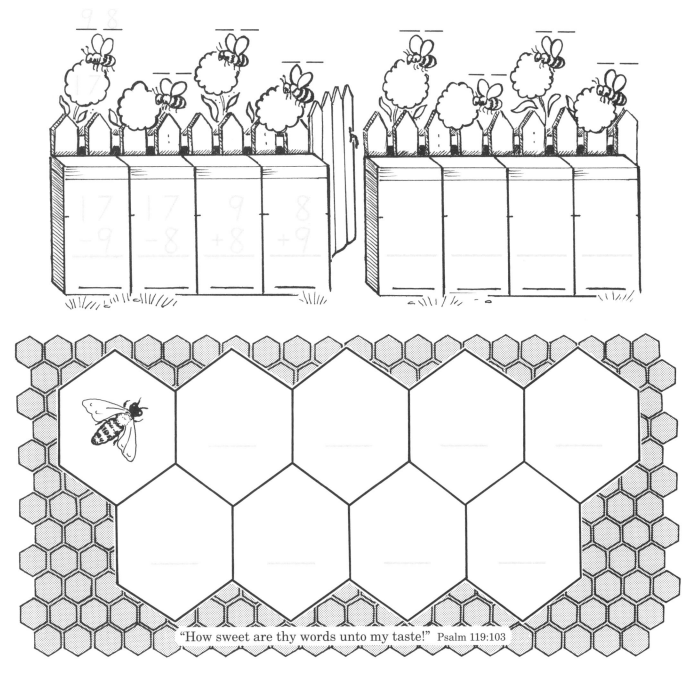

"How sweet are thy words unto my taste!" Psalm 119:103

179 -94	178 -86	83 +96	179 -86
78 +79	179 -82	69 +78	176 -94
78 +99	179 -87	178 -94	96 +83
178 -85	93 +85	178 -96	88 +59
176 -83	94 +85	177 -85	177 -92
69 +28	179 -87	95 +84	179 -95

92 +86	177 -84
177 -85	58 +39
177 -80	69 +88
77 +98	179 -98
177 -85	79 +98

Fred has 59¢ in his bank. Lee has 38¢ in his bank. How many cents do both boys have?

17 bees buzz inside red tulips. Then 8 bees fly back to the hive. How many bees are still inside red tulips?

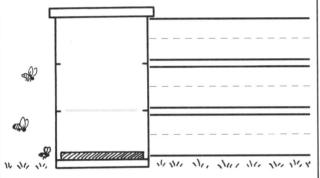

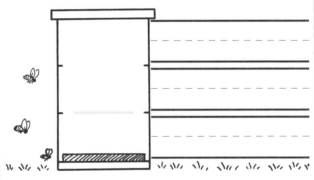

2 cups   =   1 pint

2 pints   =   1 quart

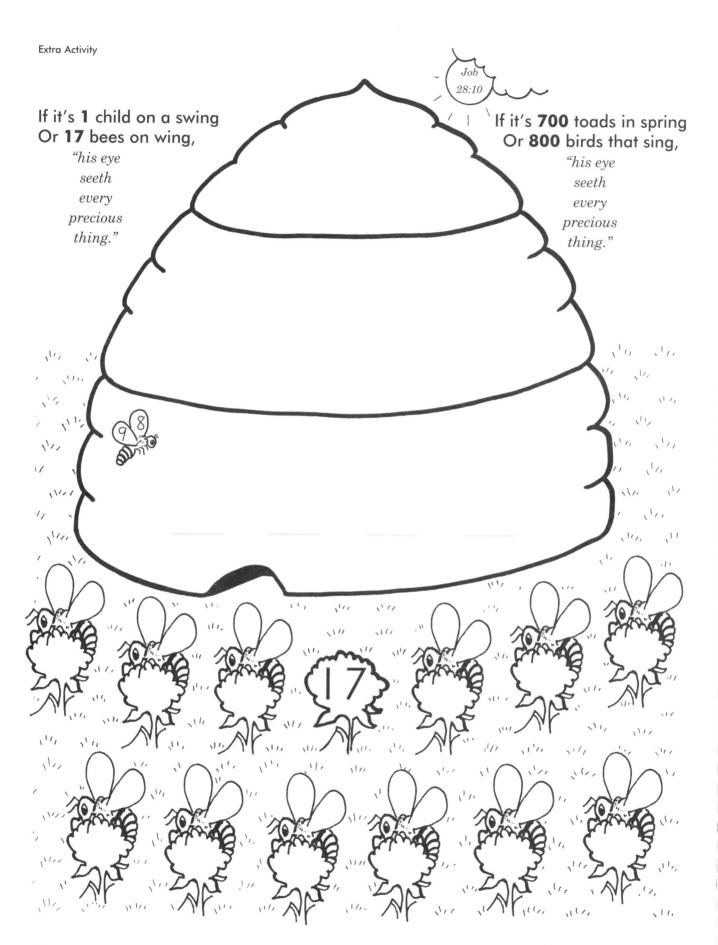

If it's **1** child on a swing
Or **17** bees on wing,
*"his eye
seeth
every
precious
thing."*

*Job
28:10*

If it's **700** toads in spring
Or **800** birds that sing,
*"his eye
seeth
every
precious
thing."*

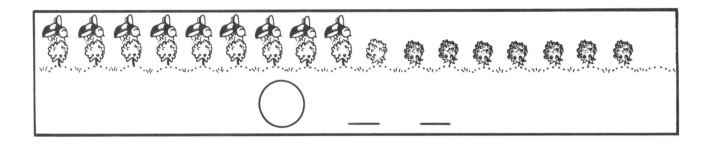

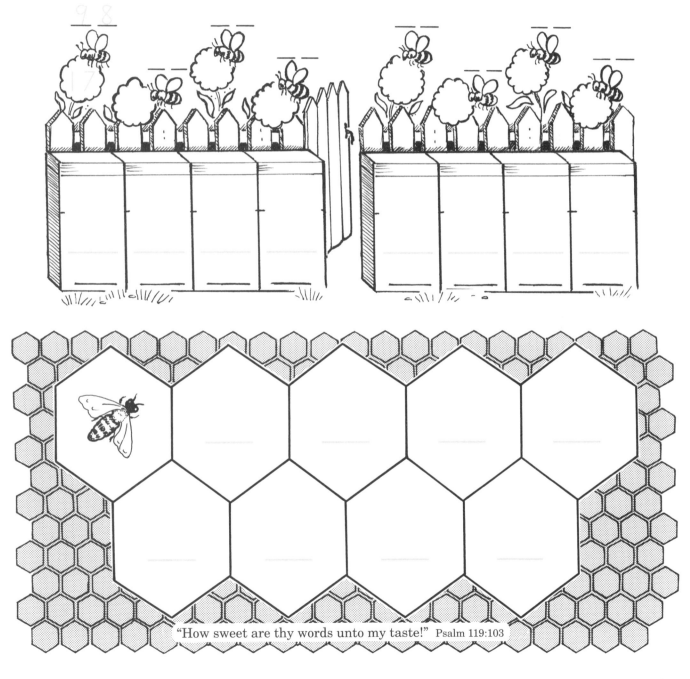

"How sweet are thy words unto my taste!" Psalm 119:103

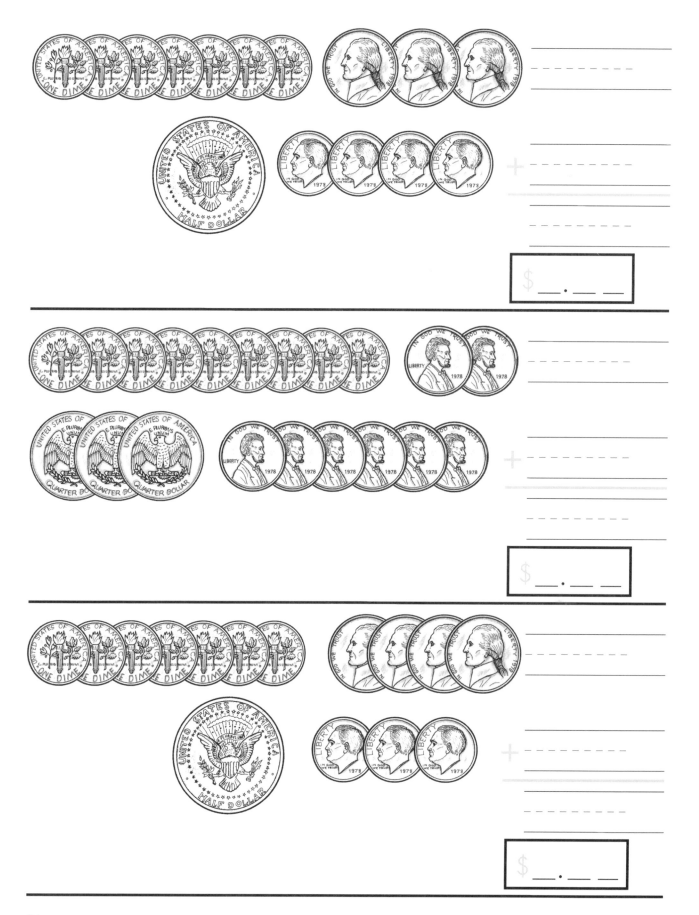

```
  97        76        88        88        97        95
 -79       -27       +79       +88       -69       -56
_____    _____    _____    _____    _____    _____


  68        76        89        87        76        97
 +99       -49       +77       -59       +89       -68
_____    _____    _____    _____    _____    _____


  87        86        67        89        87        85
 -68       -38       +99       +88       -58       -47
_____    _____    _____    _____    _____    _____
```

2 cups   =   1 pint

2 pints   =   1 quart

Speed
Drill

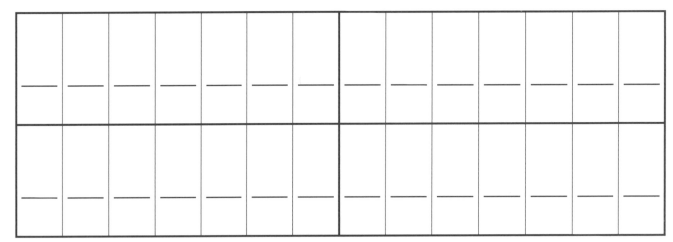

17	17	9	16	16	8
-9	-8	+7	-9	-7	+9

9	16	17	17	7	16
+8	-7	-8	-9	+9	-7

9	16	8	17	16	9	17	17
+8	-7	+9	-8	-9	+7	-8	-9

17	9	16	7	17	17	16	8
-8	+8	-7	+9	-9	-8	-7	+9

"Whatsoever thy hand findeth to do, do it with thy might." Ecclesiastes 9:10

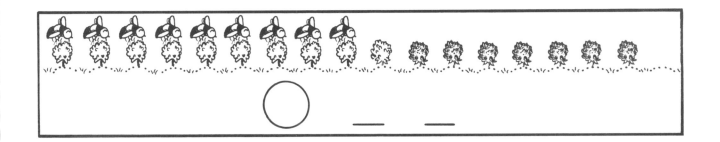

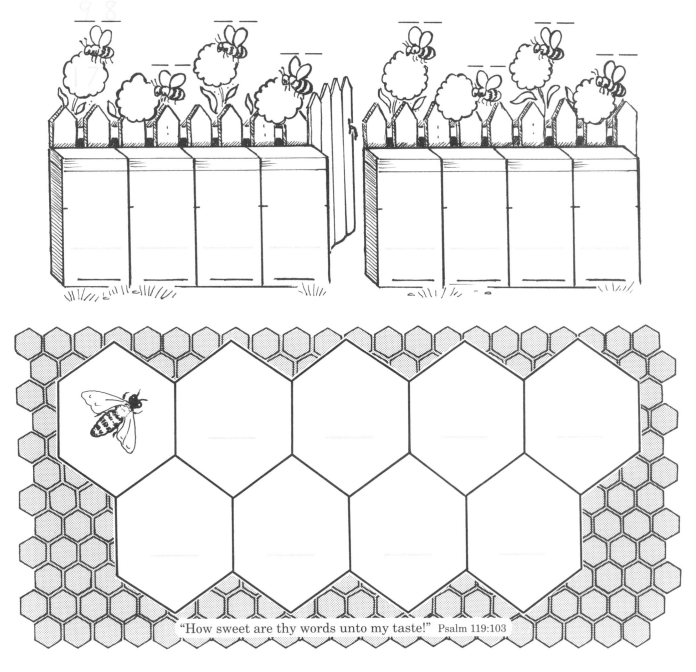

"How sweet are thy words unto my taste!" Psalm 119:103

$9 + \underline{} = 17$	$17 - \underline{} = 8$	$\underline{} - 8 = 9$
$8 + \underline{} = 17$	$\underline{} + 9 = 17$	$8 + \underline{} = 17$
$17 - \underline{} = 9$	$\underline{} - 9 = 8$	$17 - 9 = \underline{}$
$17 - \underline{} = 8$	$17 - 8 = \underline{}$	$\underline{} - 8 = 9$
$\underline{} + 9 = 17$	$8 + \underline{} = 17$	$8 + \underline{} = 17$
$\underline{} - 9 = 8$	$9 + 8 = \underline{}$	$\underline{} - 9 = 8$

$$
\begin{array}{cccccccc}
6 & 7 & 1 & 4 & 8 & 5 & 7 & 6 \\
3 & 2 & 7 & 5 & 1 & 2 & 2 & 2 \\
+8 & +5 & +9 & +8 & +7 & +8 & +8 & +9 \\
\hline
\end{array}
$$

$$
\begin{array}{cccccccc}
5 & 2 & 2 & 4 & 5 & 1 & 1 & 4 \\
4 & 6 & 7 & 3 & 3 & 8 & 6 & 4 \\
+8 & +9 & +6 & +9 & +9 & +8 & +7 & +9 \\
\hline
\end{array}
$$

```
  39        97        99        76        97        66
 +38       -78       +67       +99       -59       -58
_____    _____    _____    _____    _____    _____


  88        97        77        95        89        96
 +89       -19       +99       -27       +86       -38
_____    _____    _____    _____    _____    _____


  96        86        78        87        77        95
 -17       -69       +87       +89       -39       -87
_____    _____    _____    _____    _____    _____
```

2 cups = 1 pint

2 pints = 1 quart

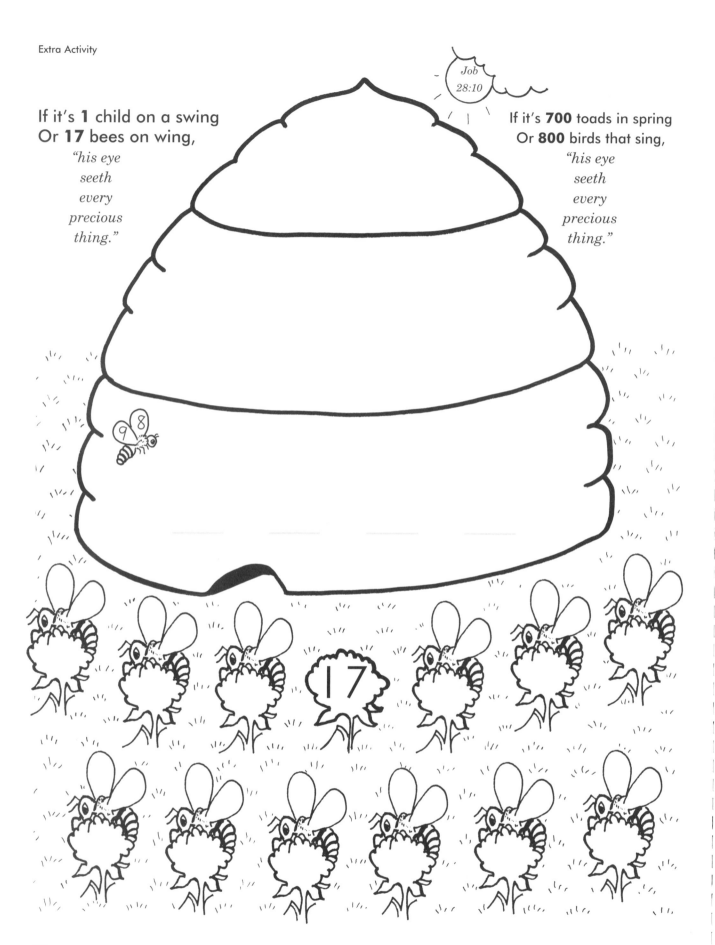

If it's **1** child on a swing
Or **17** bees on wing,

"his eye
seeth
every
precious
thing."

Job 28:10

If it's **700** toads in spring
Or **800** birds that sing,

"his eye
seeth
every
precious
thing."

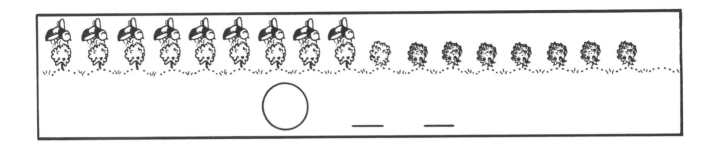

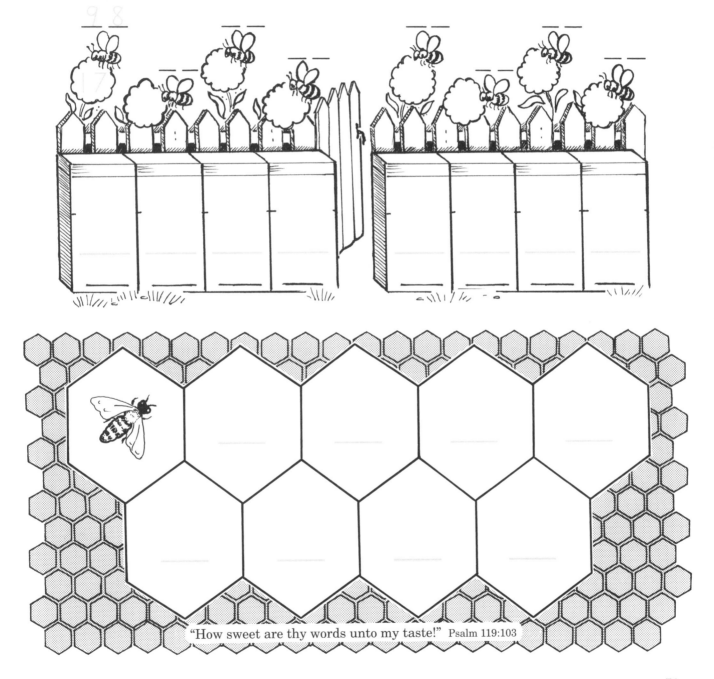

"How sweet are thy words unto my taste!" Psalm 119:103

Seventeen children are in Ray's Sunday school class. Nine children are boys. How many children are girls?

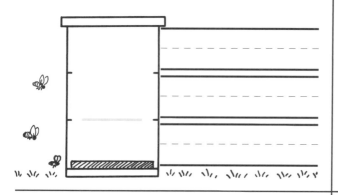

Little lambs run and skip. 19 lambs are black. 18 lambs are white. How many lambs is that altogether?

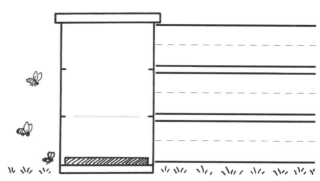

Mother plants one dozen plants in the garden and 29 plants in the flower bed. How many plants is that?

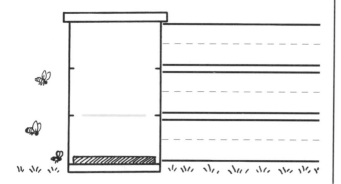

Seventeen bees buzz. Then a toad eats 8 of them. How many bees are left?

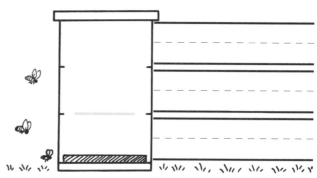

```
  97        95        96        99        76        95
 -79       -78       -38       -56       -49       -56
_____    _____    _____    _____    _____    _____


  97        86        87        96        77        77
 -67       -39       -58       -48       -49       -28
_____    _____    _____    _____    _____    _____


  67        84        54        96        78        55
 -28       -26       -37       -69       -35       -37
_____    _____    _____    _____    _____    _____
```

4 quarts = 1 gallon

Speed
Drill

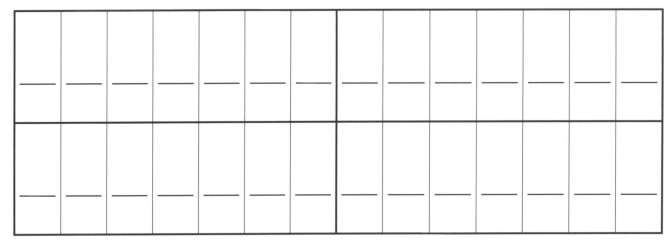

7	9	17	16	8	17
+9	+8	−8	−7	+8	−9

16	17	9	8	16	16
−7	−9	+7	+9	−8	−7

17	9	17	8	16	17	9	9
−9	+8	−9	+8	−7	−8	+8	+7

8	16	17	17	8	7	17	16
+9	−8	−8	−9	+9	+9	−9	−7

"Whatsoever thy hand findeth to do, do it with thy might." Ecclesiastes 9:10

74

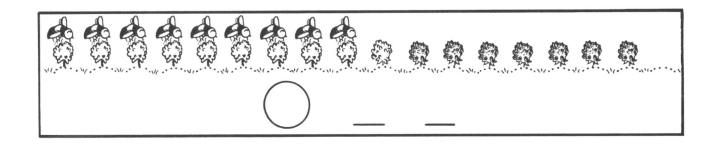

$\bigcirc$ ___ ___

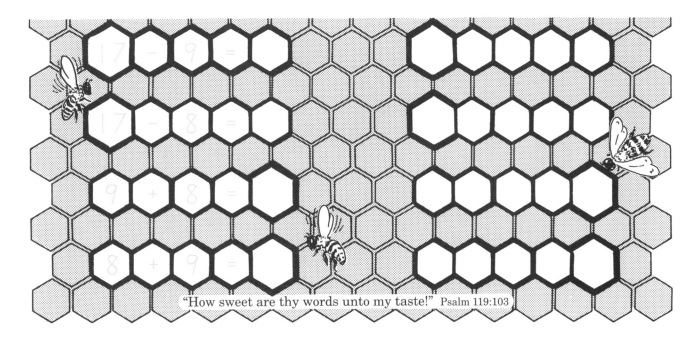

$17 - 9 =$

$17 - 8 =$

$9 + 8 =$

$8 + 9 =$

"How sweet are thy words unto my taste!" Psalm 119:103

$$
\begin{array}{cccccc}
17 & 9 & 17 & 8 & 16 & 16 \\
-9 & +8 & -8 & +9 & -9 & -7 \\
\hline
\end{array}
$$

$$
\begin{array}{cccccccc}
17 & 17 & 7 & 16 & 8 & 9 & 17 & 17 \\
-8 & -9 & +9 & -7 & +9 & +7 & -9 & -9 \\
\hline
\end{array}
$$

$$
\begin{array}{cccccccc}
7 & 17 & 16 & 16 & 8 & 16 & 17 & 17 \\
+9 & -9 & -7 & -9 & +9 & -7 & -9 & -8 \\
\hline
\end{array}
$$

$$
\begin{array}{cccccccc}
17 & 8 & 16 & 9 & 16 & 16 & 9 & 9 \\
-8 & +9 & -7 & +8 & -9 & -7 & +8 & +7 \\
\hline
\end{array}
$$

$$
\begin{array}{cccccccc}
17 & 17 & 16 & 7 & 17 & 16 & 17 & 9 \\
-8 & -9 & -9 & +9 & -9 & -9 & -9 & +8 \\
\hline
\end{array}
$$

$$
\begin{array}{cccccccc}
8 & 7 & 17 & 17 & 9 & 17 & 9 & 17 \\
+9 & +9 & -8 & -9 & +7 & -8 & +7 & -8 \\
\hline
\end{array}
$$

```
  35      47      15      64      45      63
  43      31      63      23      22      23
 +79     +69     +96     +69     +78     +78
_____   _____   _____   _____   _____   _____


  65      45      32      53      40      36
  24      22      56      22      49      53
 +78     +93     +28     +95     +78     +28
_____   _____   _____   _____   _____   _____


  24      35      45      63      43      23
  54      23      34      22      45      34
 +96     +87     +78     +79     +59     +99
_____   _____   _____   _____   _____   _____
```

4 quarts = 1 gallon

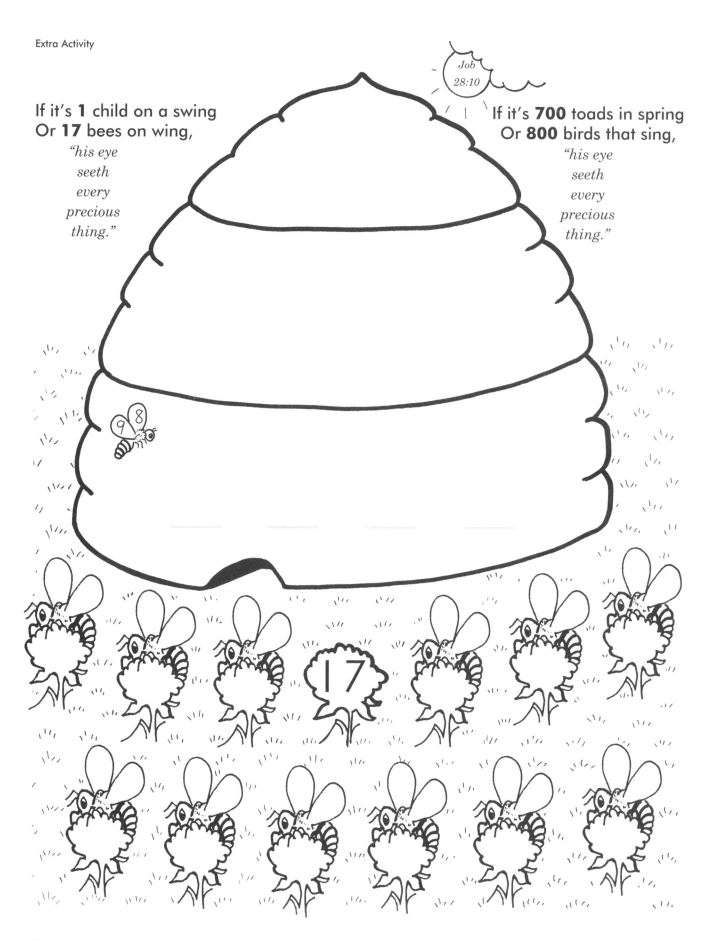

If it's **1** child on a swing
Or **17** bees on wing,

*"his eye
seeth
every
precious
thing."*

*Job
28:10*

If it's **700** toads in spring
Or **800** birds that sing,

*"his eye
seeth
every
precious
thing."*

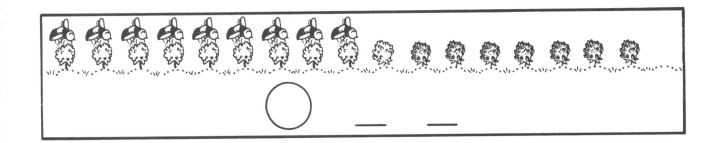

$$\bigcirc \qquad \underline{\quad} \quad \underline{\quad}$$

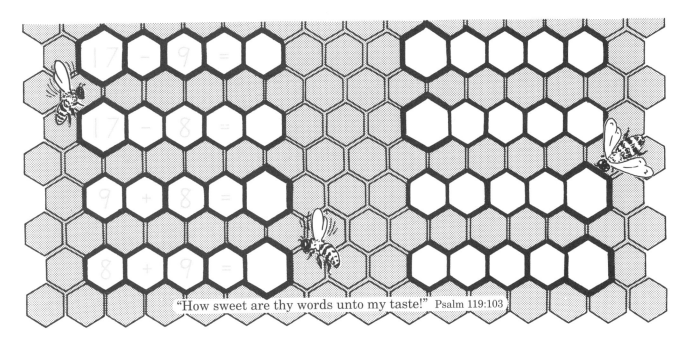

"How sweet are thy words unto my taste!" Psalm 119:103

17 -8	9 +8	15 -6	8 +9	14 -5	9 +7

8 +8	6 +9	7 +7	14 -5	8 +9	6 +8	7 +8	16 -7

7 +9	16 -8	15 -6	15 -9	8 +7	17 -8	14 -6	17 -9

15 -7	8 +6	16 -9	9 +6	14 -8	15 -8	9 +5	9 +7

16 -9	17 -9	17 -8	6 +8	15 -7	16 -7	16 -8	6 +9

7 +8	9 +8	14 -7	17 -9	5 +9	16 -9	8 +9	15 -8

80

97	76	78	77	95	97
-58	-58	+89	+69	-48	-69

58	86	87	94	58	76
+99	-79	+69	-77	+97	-49

85	95	68	59	87	85
-47	-76	+98	+88	-39	-58

4 quarts = 1 gallon

Speed
Drill

9	7	9	8	8	8
+8	+9	+6	+9	+9	+8

8	8	8	6	9	9
+7	+9	+8	+8	+8	+7

7	8	7	9	8	9	7	9
+8	+9	+9	+8	+9	+6	+9	+8

3	4	6	4	3	7	4	5
5	2	2	5	4	2	4	3
+9	+9	+8	+8	+7	+7	+9	+7

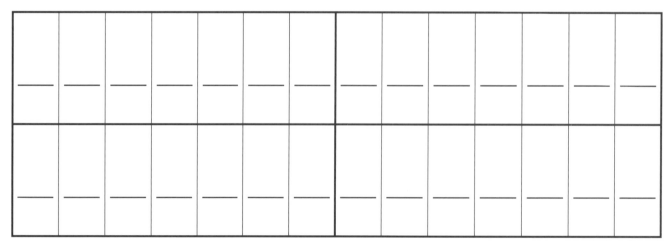

"Whatsoever thy hand findeth to do, do it with thy might." Ecclesiastes 9:10

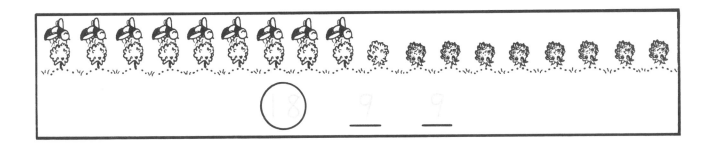

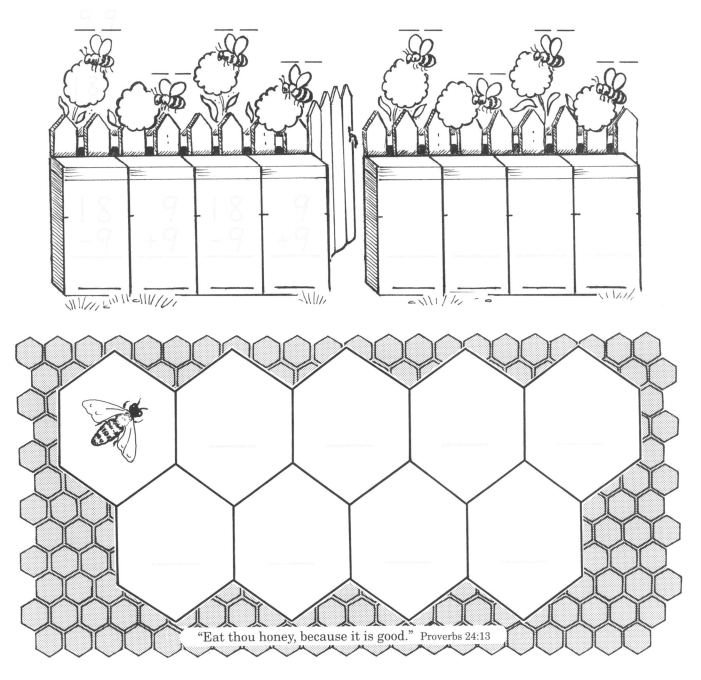

"Eat thou honey, because it is good." Proverbs 24:13

18	9	17	9			18	17
-9	+9	-8	+8			-9	-9

9	9	17	18	8	17	9	18
+9	+9	-9	-9	+9	-8	+9	-9

8	17	18	18	9	9	18	17
+9	-9	-9	-9	+9	+8	-9	-8

17	18	9	9	18	18	17	8
-8	-9	+8	+9	-9	-9	-9	+9

18	17	18				18	17	9
-9	-8	-9				-9	-9	+9

17	8	9	17	18	18	17	18
-8	+9	+9	-9	-9	-9	-8	-9

183	368	259	468	149	487
+597	+526	+179	+399	+629	+198

438	317	558	448	318	649
+267	+659	+148	+529	+389	+329

286	229	589	149	276	586
+399	+549	+278	+289	+618	+194

16 ounces = 1 pound

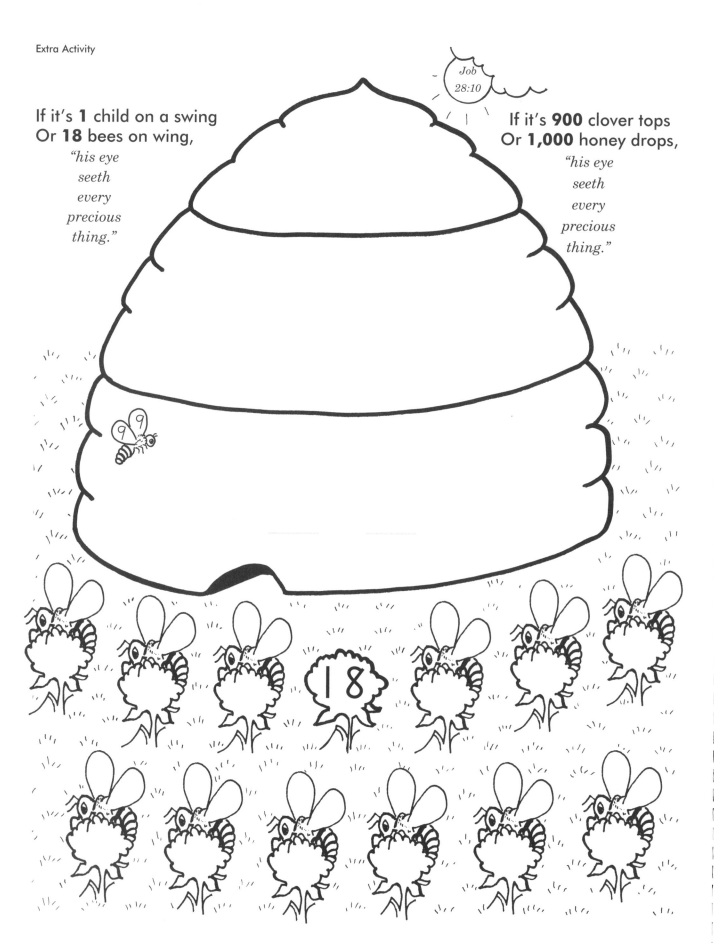

If it's **1** child on a swing
Or **18** bees on wing,
"his eye
seeth
every
precious
thing."

Job 28:10

If it's **900** clover tops
Or **1,000** honey drops,
"his eye
seeth
every
precious
thing."

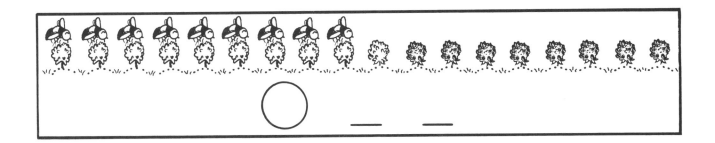

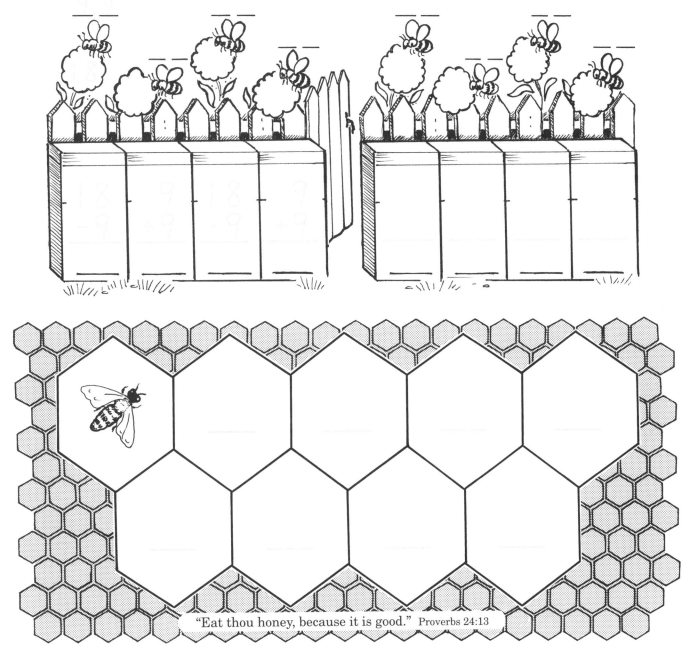

"Eat thou honey, because it is good." Proverbs 24:13

87

```
   91        183        83                          58
  +92        -92       +94                         +39
_____   _____   _____                    _____


  179        189        49        178        96        189
  -87        -93       +39        -94       +80        -95
_____   _____   _____   _____   _____   _____


   95        184        68         95        189        93
  +94        -94       +29        +82        -98       +90
_____   _____   _____   _____   _____   _____


  188        177        188        81        189        86
  -95        -94        -97       +97        -97       +93
_____   _____   _____   _____   _____   _____


  178        29                              178        189
  -94        +59                             -82        -97
_____   _____                         _____   _____


   91        187        89        189        179        185
  +88        -95       +89        -98        -96        -92
_____   _____   _____   _____   _____   _____
```

18	9	17	7	9	8	15	16
-9	+9	-9	+9	+8	+7	-6	-7

8	15	16	9	18	17	7	15
+9	-6	-8	+8	-9	-9	+8	-8

9	18	9	15	6	8	15	16
+9	-9	+7	-7	+9	+9	-6	-7

16 ounces = 1 pound

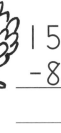

Speed Drill

17	18	16	18	16	15
-9	-9	-9	-9	-7	-9

15	17	15	17	18	16
-8	-8	-7	-9	-9	-9

16	18	15	18	17	15	16	17
-7	-9	-9	-9	-8	-8	-7	-9

5	6	5	2	6	3	4	3
4	2	3	7	3	4	5	6
+9	+9	+8	+9	+9	+9	+8	+9

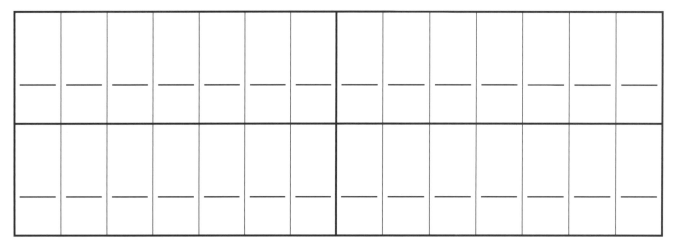

"Whatsoever thy hand findeth to do, do it with thy might." Ecclesiastes 9:10

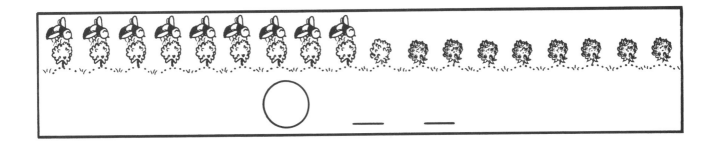

$$\bigcirc \quad \underline{\quad} \quad \underline{\quad}$$

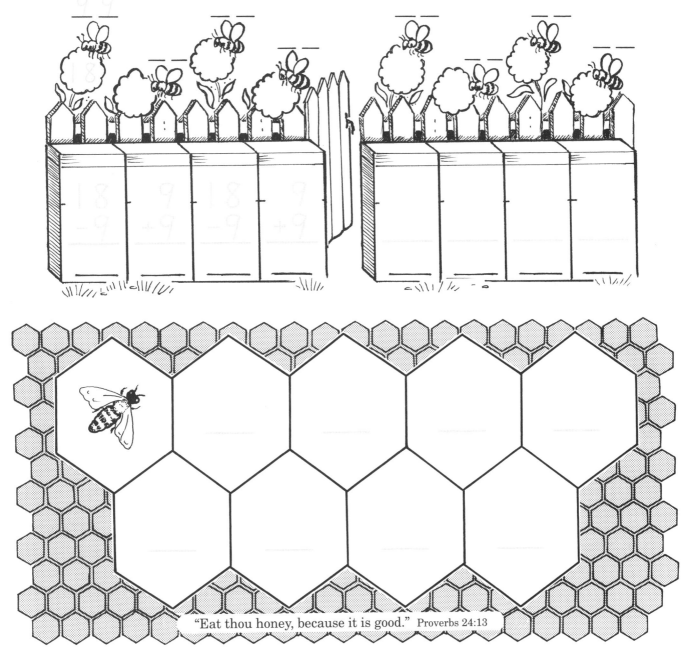

"Eat thou honey, because it is good." Proverbs 24:13

Mae and Fay played store. Mae sold a cup for 59¢ and a bell for 39¢. How many cents was that altogether?

Mother made one dozen muffins. She gave seven muffins to Grandmother and kept the rest. How many did she keep?

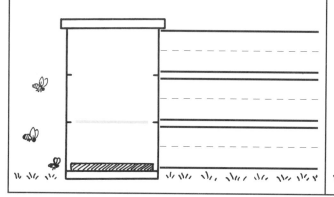
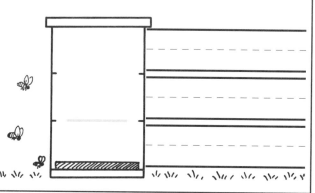

6	7	3	8	2	4	3	6
3	2	5	1	4	5	4	1
+9	+6	+8	+9	+9	+6	+9	+7

7	2	2	4	2	6	4	1
2	6	4	5	5	1	2	5
+9	+8	+9	+9	+7	+9	+9	+9

```
  98        39        87        85        49        98
 -59       +47       -48       -28       +58       -69
_____     _____     _____     _____     _____     _____


  57        37        76        95        27        86
 -19       +59       -39       -58       +69       -48
_____     _____     _____     _____     _____     _____


  28        78        96        96        88        38
 +58       -39       -39       -57       -59       +69
_____     _____     _____     _____     _____     _____
```

16 ounces = 1 pound

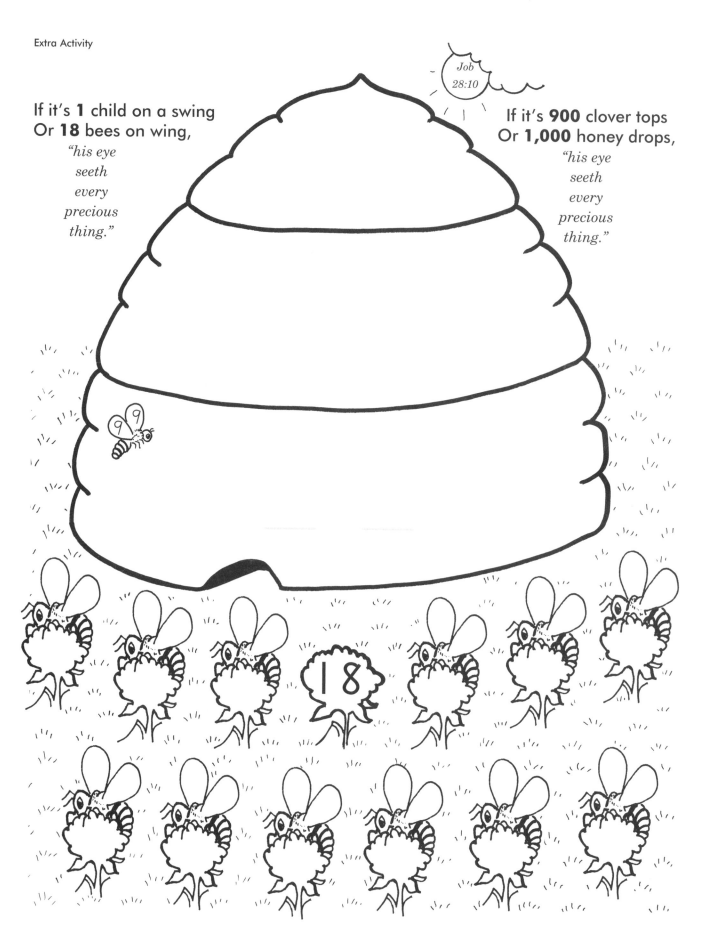

If it's **1** child on a swing
Or **18** bees on wing,

*"his eye
seeth
every
precious
thing."*

Job
28:10

If it's **900** clover tops
Or **1,000** honey drops,

*"his eye
seeth
every
precious
thing."*

9	11	8	18	11	17	9	16
+2	-6	+7	-9	-9	-8	+7	-8

8	11	9	16	15	2	16	17
+9	-2	+9	-7	-8	+9	-9	-9

15	9	17	9	15	11	8	15
-6	+9	-8	+8	-7	-4	+3	-8

11	17	11	16	9	16	6	15
-8	-9	-8	-8	+6	-9	+9	-8

11	7	18	11	16	8	11
-6	+8	-9	-9	-7	+8	-3

7	15	5	11	11	6	11
+4	-9	+6	-5	-7	+5	-7

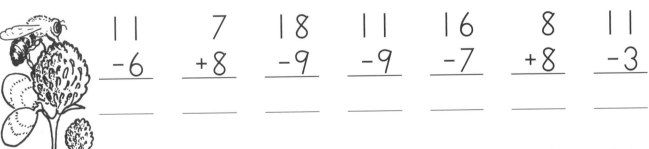

114 -93	93 +22	156 -94	175 -91	86 +84	118 -66

36 +83	169 -98	92 +75	187 -94	35 +66	167 -82

24 +91	118 -97	117 -33	117 -55	119 -67	83 +87

117 -46	47 +72	158 -65	74 +93	159 -74	27 +74

89 +86	158 -88	78 +37	77 +88	178 -83

165 -70	69 +96	66 +49	165 -95	77 +98

	thousands	hundreds	tens	ones
1583	___	___	___	___
1815	___	___	___	___
80	___	___	___	___
293	___	___	___	___
1325	___	___	___	___
1324	___	___	___	___
1623	___	___	___	___

	thousands	hundreds	tens	ones
1639	___	___	___	___
1298	___	___	___	___
20	___	___	___	___
1315	___	___	___	___
290	___	___	___	___
1784	___	___	___	___
1816	___	___	___	___

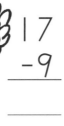

Speed Drill

9 +9	18 -9	17 -8	9 +8	17 -9	8 +9

17 -9	9 +9	17 -8	9 +8	8 +9	17 -8

8 +9	9 +9	8 +9	17 -9	9 +8	18 -9	17 -8	9 +9

5 4 +9	2 6 +9	2 7 +9	3 5 +9	8 1 +9	4 5 +9	6 3 +8	7 2 +9

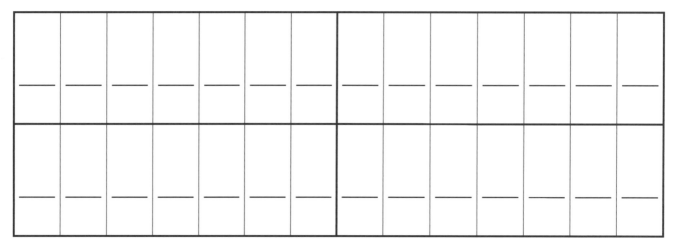

"Whatsoever thy hand findeth to do, do it with thy might." Ecclesiastes 9:10

3 +8	11 -7	8 +7	18 -9	11 -3	17 -8	9 +7	11 -9

8 +9	17 -8	9 +9	15 -6	15 -8	4 +7	16 -9	17 -9

16 -7	9 +9	11 -2	9 +8	15 -7	16 -9	8 +3	15 -8

16 -8	11 -8	17 -9	11 -8	9 +6	11 -4	6 +9	15 -8

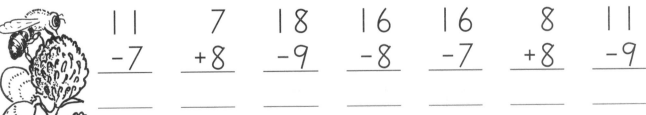

11 -7	7 +8	18 -9	16 -8	16 -7	8 +8	11 -9

7 +4	11 -5	5 +6	15 -9	11 -6	6 +5	11 -6

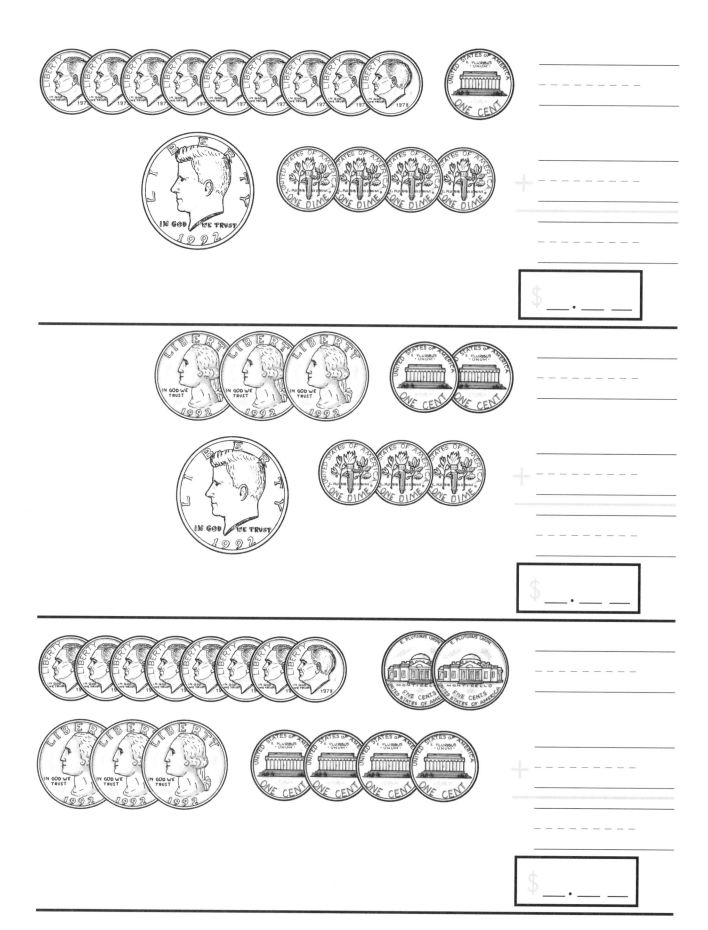

```
  80      97      59      58      68      71
 -54     -78     +48     +38     -49     -45
 ____    ____    ____    ____    ____    ____
```

```
  28      85      27      88      97      36
 +77     -27     +69     +19     -39     +69
 ____    ____    ____    ____    ____    ____
```

```
 16    9    17     7     9     8    15    17
 -7   +9    -9    +9    +8    +7   -6    -8
 __    __   __    __    __    __   __    __
```

```
  8    17    18     9    16    15     7    15
 +9    -9    -9    +8    -8    -6    +8    -8
 __    __    __    __    __    __    __    __
```

```
  9    18     9    15     6     8    15    16
 +9    -9    +7    -7    +9    +9    -6    -7
 __    __    __    __    __    __    __    __
```

5 +7	12 -7	17 -8	9 +9	12 -8	8 +9	12 -5	12 -9
17 -8	6 +6	18 -9	9 +3	16 -8	8 +9	9 +8	17 -9
12 -9	15 -8	9 +8	12 -8	9 +9	15 -6	12 -7	8 +4
12 -6	3 +9	16 -8	17 -9	12 -4	16 -9	4 +8	16 -7
7 +8	15 -6	6 +9	16 -7	9 +6	7 +9	8 +8	8 +7

16 -9	15 -7	17 -9	12 -4	7 +5	15 -9

103

```
 126        88       166       158        66       168
 -95       +37       -94       -65       +96       -86
_____     _____     _____     _____     _____     _____


  86       179        88       127        93       189
 +83       -88       +64       -84       +75       -96
_____     _____     _____     _____     _____     _____


  47       129       127       159       156        67
 +78       -98       -34       -87       -74       +95
_____     _____     _____     _____     _____     _____


 167        95       128        84       187        73
 -76       +74       -85       +68       -94       +95
_____     _____     _____     _____     _____     _____


 129        26       128        88        69       128
 -65       +99       -48       +69       +98       -63
_____     _____     _____     _____     _____     _____
```

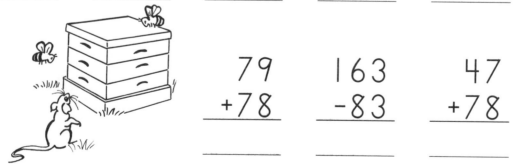

```
            79       163        47       158
           +78       -83       +78       -94
          _____     _____     _____     _____
```

```
 34     44     25     53     35     64
 43     30     43     33     22     25
+79    +98    +99    +99    +28    +78
____   ____   ____   ____   ____   ____


 46     39     33     54     43     36
 43     50     54     34     25     53
+68    +86    +78    +99    +14    +77
____   ____   ____   ____   ____   ____
```

12 inches = 1 foot

_____   _____
- - - - - - - -   - - - - - - - -
_____   _____

3 feet = 1 yard

_____   _____
- - - - - - - -   - - - - - - - -
_____   _____

16 ounces = 1 pound

_____   _____
- - - - - - - -   - - - - - - - -
_____   _____

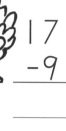

Speed
Drill

9 +7	17 −9	9 +9	16 −9	9 +8	7 +9

17 −9	8 +9	16 −7	18 −9	9 +8	17 −9

7 +9	8 +9	16 −9	9 +9	17 −9	9 +7	9 +8	18 −9

6 2 +9	3 6 +7	5 4 +9	4 4 +9	7 2 +8	8 1 +9	4 3 +9	5 3 +9

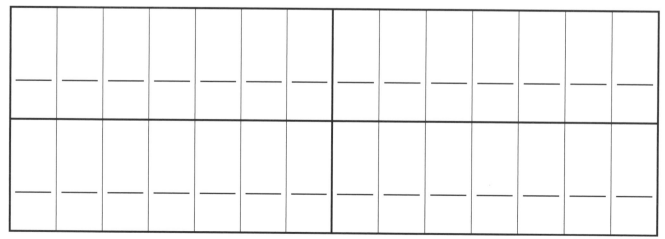

"Whatsoever thy hand findeth to do, do it with thy might." Ecclesiastes 9:10

$$\begin{array}{r} 8 \\ +4 \\ \hline \end{array} \quad \begin{array}{r} 12 \\ -9 \\ \hline \end{array} \quad \begin{array}{r} 15 \\ -6 \\ \hline \end{array} \quad \begin{array}{r} 9 \\ +9 \\ \hline \end{array} \quad \begin{array}{r} 12 \\ -8 \\ \hline \end{array} \quad \begin{array}{r} 8 \\ +9 \\ \hline \end{array} \quad \begin{array}{r} 15 \\ -8 \\ \hline \end{array} \quad \begin{array}{r} 12 \\ -7 \\ \hline \end{array}$$

$$\begin{array}{r} 18 \\ -9 \\ \hline \end{array} \quad \begin{array}{r} 9 \\ +3 \\ \hline \end{array} \quad \begin{array}{r} 17 \\ -8 \\ \hline \end{array} \quad \begin{array}{r} 6 \\ +6 \\ \hline \end{array} \quad \begin{array}{r} 16 \\ -8 \\ \hline \end{array} \quad \begin{array}{r} 8 \\ +9 \\ \hline \end{array} \quad \begin{array}{r} 9 \\ +8 \\ \hline \end{array} \quad \begin{array}{r} 17 \\ -9 \\ \hline \end{array}$$

$$\begin{array}{r} 12 \\ -7 \\ \hline \end{array} \quad \begin{array}{r} 12 \\ -5 \\ \hline \end{array} \quad \begin{array}{r} 9 \\ +8 \\ \hline \end{array} \quad \begin{array}{r} 12 \\ -8 \\ \hline \end{array} \quad \begin{array}{r} 9 \\ +9 \\ \hline \end{array} \quad \begin{array}{r} 17 \\ -8 \\ \hline \end{array} \quad \begin{array}{r} 12 \\ -9 \\ \hline \end{array} \quad \begin{array}{r} 5 \\ +7 \\ \hline \end{array}$$

$$\begin{array}{r} 15 \\ -9 \\ \hline \end{array} \quad \begin{array}{r} 7 \\ +5 \\ \hline \end{array} \quad \begin{array}{r} 16 \\ -8 \\ \hline \end{array} \quad \begin{array}{r} 17 \\ -9 \\ \hline \end{array} \quad \begin{array}{r} 15 \\ -7 \\ \hline \end{array} \quad \begin{array}{r} 16 \\ -9 \\ \hline \end{array} \quad \begin{array}{r} 4 \\ +8 \\ \hline \end{array} \quad \begin{array}{r} 16 \\ -7 \\ \hline \end{array}$$

$$\begin{array}{r} 6 \\ +9 \\ \hline \end{array} \quad \begin{array}{r} 15 \\ -6 \\ \hline \end{array} \quad \begin{array}{r} 8 \\ +7 \\ \hline \end{array} \quad \begin{array}{r} 16 \\ -7 \\ \hline \end{array} \quad \begin{array}{r} 9 \\ +6 \\ \hline \end{array} \quad \begin{array}{r} 7 \\ +9 \\ \hline \end{array} \quad \begin{array}{r} 8 \\ +8 \\ \hline \end{array} \quad \begin{array}{r} 8 \\ +7 \\ \hline \end{array}$$

$$\begin{array}{r} 16 \\ -9 \\ \hline \end{array} \quad \begin{array}{r} 12 \\ -4 \\ \hline \end{array} \quad \begin{array}{r} 17 \\ -9 \\ \hline \end{array} \quad \begin{array}{r} 12 \\ -4 \\ \hline \end{array} \quad \begin{array}{r} 3 \\ +9 \\ \hline \end{array} \quad \begin{array}{r} 12 \\ -6 \\ \hline \end{array}$$

$9 + \underline{} = 18$	$16 - \underline{} = 9$	$\underline{} - 7 = 8$
$9 + \underline{} = 17$	$\underline{} + 8 = 15$	$9 + \underline{} = 18$
$16 - \underline{} = 8$	$\underline{} - 9 = 9$	$15 - 7 = \underline{}$
$15 - \underline{} = 9$	$17 - 8 = \underline{}$	$\underline{} - 8 = 9$
$\underline{} + 9 = 16$	$9 + \underline{} = 18$	$8 + \underline{} = 16$
$\underline{} - 9 = 6$	$9 + 7 = \underline{}$	$\underline{} - 9 = 7$

$$
\begin{array}{cccccccc}
6 & 3 & 4 & 3 & 8 & 2 & 4 & 7 \\
3 & 5 & 5 & 5 & 1 & 7 & 3 & 1 \\
+7 & +7 & +9 & +9 & +8 & +7 & +8 & +8 \\
\hline
\end{array}
$$

$$
\begin{array}{cccccccc}
5 & 3 & 7 & 3 & 5 & 2 & 1 & 4 \\
4 & 6 & 2 & 6 & 3 & 5 & 6 & 4 \\
+8 & +9 & +6 & +7 & +8 & +8 & +9 & +9 \\
\hline
\end{array}
$$

163

38 +69	56 -48	29 +77	98 -59	48 +54	76 -47
86 -59	79 +79	75 -49	59 +98	50 -25	89 +67
95 -87	79 +28	78 -39	37 +69	57 -28	65 +37

Write $\frac{1}{2}$ on each **half**.

Write $\frac{1}{4}$ on each **fourth**.

Write $\frac{1}{3}$ on each **third**.

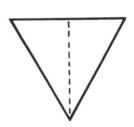

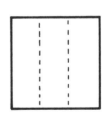

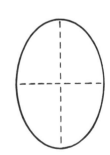

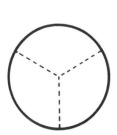

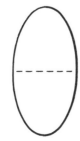

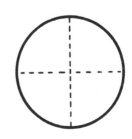

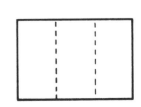

109

13	13	15	13	7	16	17	5
-9	-4	-8	-7	+6	-9	-8	+8

4	17	9	6	15	8	16	13
+9	-9	+8	+7	-9	+9	-8	-9

17	15	9	13	7	7	13	8
-9	-7	+6	-8	+9	+8	-5	+5

9	8	13	9	13	16	7	17
+4	+8	-6	+7	-8	-9	+9	-9

18	16	17	18	15	15	17	6
-9	-8	-9	-9	-6	-7	-9	+9

8	15	16	16	9	16
+7	-6	-7	-7	+9	-7

111

```
 136      38      167     156      56     138
 -86     +45      -85     -94     +83     -46
_____   _____    _____   _____   _____   _____


  38     179      65     179      37     159
 +69     -96     +85     -84     +26     -81
_____   _____    _____   _____   _____   _____


  56     138     135     135     189      44
 +27     -88     -73     -53     -97     +95
_____   _____    _____   _____   _____   _____


 158      59     157      56     168      39
 -75     +48     -62     +94     -90     +24
_____   _____    _____   _____   _____   _____


 168      82     178      79      64     139
 -73     +82     -94     +26     +96     -98
_____   _____    _____   _____   _____   _____
```

```
          88     167      91     187
         +17     -83     +73     -92
        _____   _____   _____   _____
```

164

Lee's family drove 88 miles to the zoo and 99 miles to the air-port. How many miles was that?

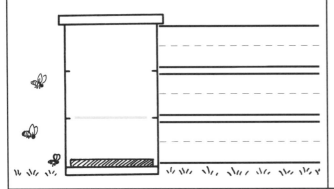

Mother made one dozen tarts. She tucked 9 tarts into lunches. How many tarts were left?

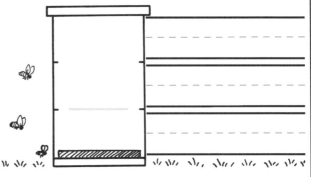

2 cups   =   1 pint

_____   _____

2 pints   =   1 quart

_____   _____

4 quarts   =   1 gallon

_____   _____

Speed
Drill

15	7	9	18	7	15
-8	+9	+9	-9	+7	-7

16	14	9	15	7	16
-9	-7	+9	-8	+8	-9

18	16	15	7	16	9	9	14
-9	-9	-7	+7	-7	+9	+7	-7

16	16	15	8	15	9	14	16
-9	-7	-8	+7	-8	+9	-7	-9

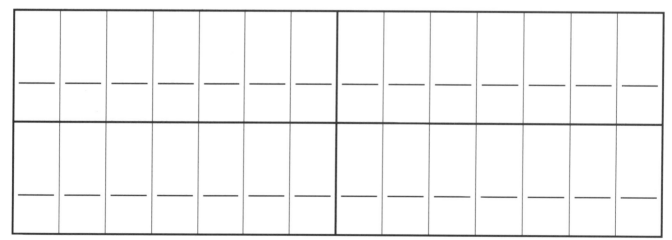

"Whatsoever thy hand findeth to do, do it with thy might." Ecclesiastes 9:10

13	17	15	15	7	16	13	4
-5	-8	-8	-9	+6	-9	-4	+9

5	17	9	6	13	8	16	17
+9	-9	+8	+7	-7	+9	-8	-9

16	17	9	13	9	7	16	9
-7	-9	+6	-8	+7	+8	-8	+4

8	8	13	7	13	16	7	18
+5	+8	-6	+9	-8	-9	+9	-9

13	13	17	16	15	15	15	6
-9	-5	-9	-7	-6	-7	-7	+9

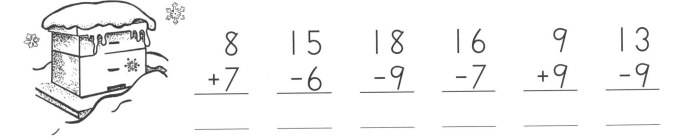

8	15	18	16	9	13
+7	-6	-9	-7	+9	-9

Father cut grass. The boys raked it into 17 heaps. They dumped 8 heaps on the garden. How many heaps were left?

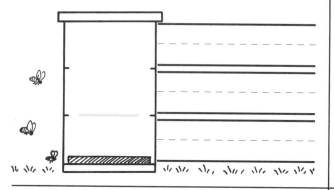

Fred and Fay played church. Fred preached for five minutes. They sang for nine minutes. How many minutes was that?

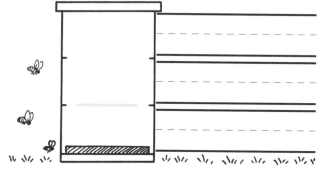

Grandfather had seventeen kids in his flock of goats. He sold eight kids. How many kids did he have then?

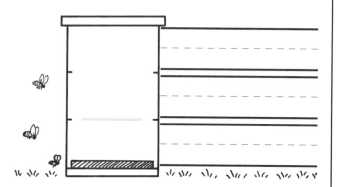

Mother has one dozen buttons in a jar and 88 buttons in a box. How many buttons does Mother have altogether?

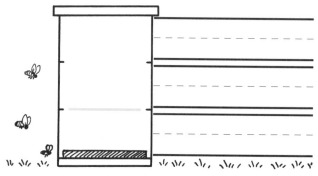

```
  68        136         37         29         97         97
 +29        -73        +46        +39        -58        -39
____       ____       ____       ____       ____       ____
```

```
  78         75         39         86         49         97
 +28        -68        +68        -18        +59        -28
____       ____       ____       ____       ____       ____
```

```
  26        159         29         15         75         86
 +67        -92        +59        +48        -37        -27
____       ____       ____       ____       ____       ____
```

14	15	14	16	9	14	16	7
−5	−7	−9	−7	+5	−9	−8	+7

5	14	9	8	14	5	15	16
+9	−7	+5	+6	−5	+9	−8	−7

14	16	7	18	9	9	15	9
−8	−9	+9	−9	+8	+7	−8	+4

4	6	14	8	17	16	7	15
+9	+8	−7	+9	−8	−9	+7	−9

17	14	9	17	17	6	15	8
−9	−8	+6	−8	−9	+9	−9	+6

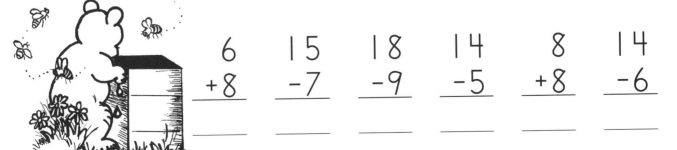

6	15	18	14	8	14
+8	−7	−9	−5	+8	−6

```
 144        35      177      146       96      168
 -93       +49      -95      -54      +53      -86
_____    _____   _____   _____   _____   _____


  38       159       75      179       69      157
 +67       -96      +85      -84      +37      -84
_____    _____   _____   _____   _____   _____


  56       149      154      145      159       74
 +28       -98      -62      -63      -77      +75
_____    _____   _____   _____   _____   _____


 148        57      187       60      146       77
 -85       +48      -92      +90      -73      +29
_____    _____   _____   _____   _____   _____


 145        96      168       79       74      149
 -95       +83      -74      +28      +66      -58
_____    _____   _____   _____   _____   _____
```

```
            88      167       84      147
           +19      -73      +95      -97
          _____   _____   _____   _____
```

120

```
  289        549        259        477        177        628
 +686       +249       +508       +379       +588       +239
 -----      -----      -----      -----      -----      -----


  489        357        358        269        167        528
 +269       +529       +399       +607       +589       +338
 -----      -----      -----      -----      -----      -----


  459        576        587        328        359        777
 +408       +189       +269       +439       +439       +198
 -----      -----      -----      -----      -----      -----
```

Write $\frac{1}{2}$ on each **half**.

Write $\frac{1}{4}$ on each **fourth**.

Write $\frac{1}{3}$ on each **third**.

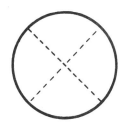

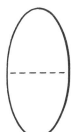
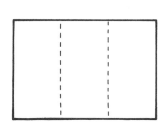
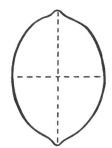
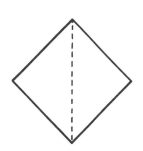
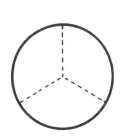

Speed
Drill

9 +8	16 −8	15 −7	8 +8	15 −8	17 −8

6 +8	8 +8	17 −9	15 −7	8 +8	8 +6

8 +9	7 +8	17 −8	15 −8	8 +8	17 −9	14 −6	9 +8

3 4 +8	4 5 +8	2 6 +8	3 5 +6	4 4 +7	7 1 +9	6 2 +8	4 2 +8

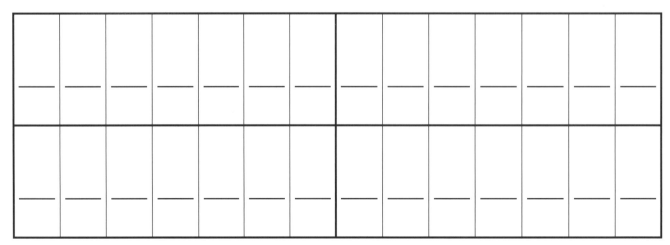

"Whatsoever thy hand findeth to do, do it with thy might." Ecclesiastes 9:10

15	14	6	14	16	8
-9	-5	+9	-7	-9	+7

9	18	7	7	17	8	15	15
+6	-9	+9	+8	-8	+8	-6	-9

17	16	8	17	8	7	14	6
-9	-7	+7	-9	+6	+8	-5	+8

7	9	15	5	14	15	7	15
+7	+7	-8	+9	-6	-8	+9	-7

14	15	15	14	9	15	15	14
-8	-7	-6	-9	+5	-6	-7	-6

16	9	9	6	14	8	9	15
-8	+9	+8	+8	-9	+9	+9	-9

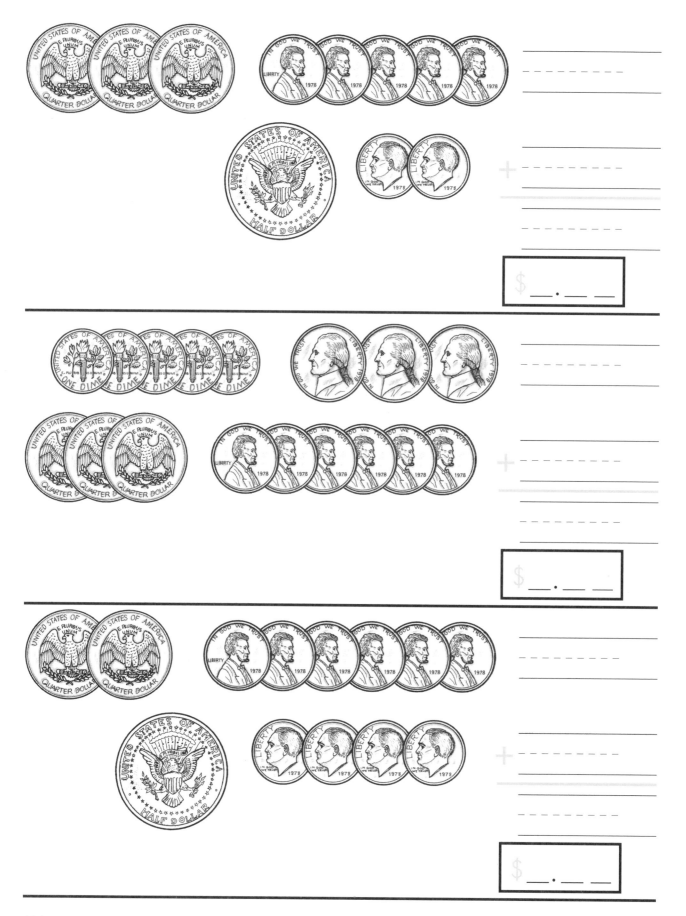

```
  94      38      87      55      39      94
 -55     +46     -48     -28     +68     -28
```

```
  55      28      74      96      47      88
 -19     +59     -37     -67     +57     -19
```

```
  75      86      97      94      85      27
 +29     -38     -39     -46     -27     +78
```

```
 18    15     9    15     8     5    17     9
 -9    -8    +6    -7    +8    +9    -8    +8
```

```
  8    15     9     7    14     8    16    14
 +9    -6    +5    +9    -6    +7    -9    -5
```

16 −9	15 −6	18 −9	9 +7	8 +6	16 −7	15 −9	9 +7
16 −8	17 −9	8 +8	16 −7	15 −8	9 +6	14 −9	6 +8
16 −7	16 −9	8 +8	14 −5	16 −7	5 +9	7 +9	14 −8
15 −7	14 −6	17 −8	7 +9	8 +7	14 −7	7 +7	14 −9
16 −8	17 −8	16 −7	7 +8	8 +9	15 −7	16 −9	9 +9

16 −8	9 +8	6 +9	15 −6	18 −9	17 −9

169 −87	68 +27	179 −94	157 −85	73 +86	166 −76
72 +74	159 −62	93 +85	156 −94	82 +66	177 −84
39 +67	149 −87	148 −74	96 +63	187 −95	57 +39
188 −95	63 +85	148 −86	84 +94	167 −70	53 +93
144 −54	84 +75	168 −96	147 −62	66 +29	156 −74
		75 +84	169 −95	147 −85	68 +38

35	46	15	64	45	63
43	31	63	23	22	26
+79	+69	+96	+69	+78	+78

55	45	32	54	23	36
24	22	56	25	45	53
+78	+78	+88	+75	+78	+78

12 inches = 1 foot

3 feet = 1 yard

16 ounces = 1 pound

129

Speed
Drill

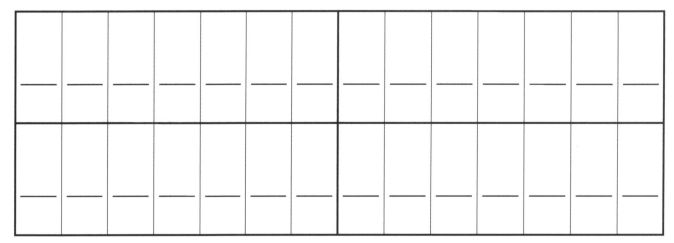

14	15	7	17	9	18
−9	−9	+9	−8	+5	−9

16	6	8	17	9	16
−9	+9	+9	−9	+9	−7

17	9	14	5	18	9	15	14
−8	+8	−5	+9	−9	+7	−9	−9

8	15	16	9	17	8	9	16
+9	−6	−7	+9	−9	+9	+6	−9

"Whatsoever thy hand findeth to do, do it with thy might." Ecclesiastes 9:10

	17	9	16	17	9	16
	−9	+8	−8	−8	+8	−9

7	7	14	8	14	15	8	17
+7	+9	−7	+9	−5	−7	+9	−9

14	6	15	9	5	9	15	17
−8	+9	−8	+7	+9	+9	−6	−8

8	14	17	7	15	17	9	15
+6	−9	−9	+8	−7	−9	+7	−6

9	15	8	16	9	6	16	18
+6	−9	+8	−9	+9	+8	−7	−9

14	9	8	14	16	14	16	7
−9	+5	+7	−6	−8	−6	−7	+9

$8 + 9 =$ ___	$15 -$ ___ $= 9$	$8 + 9 =$ ___
$15 - 6 =$ ___	$17 - 8 =$ ___	$18 - 9 =$ ___
$18 -$ ___ $= 9$	$8 + 8 =$ ___	___ $- 6 = 9$
___ $+ 8 = 15$	$9 +$ ___ $= 17$	$7 + 9 =$ ___
$15 -$ ___ $= 7$	___ $+ 6 = 15$	$8 +$ ___ $= 16$
___ $+ 7 = 16$	$16 -$ ___ $= 8$	___ $- 7 = 8$

$$
\begin{array}{cccccccc}
4 & 7 & 4 & 2 & 4 & 8 & 3 & 6 \\
4 & 2 & 3 & 6 & 5 & 0 & 3 & 3 \\
+7 & +9 & +8 & +8 & +7 & +9 & +9 & +8 \\
\hline
\end{array}
$$

$$
\begin{array}{cccccccc}
8 & 3 & 6 & 6 & 5 & 1 & 3 & 3 \\
1 & 4 & 3 & 1 & 3 & 8 & 6 & 5 \\
+7 & +8 & +9 & +8 & +9 & +6 & +8 & +8 \\
\hline
\end{array}
$$

```
   35        95        27        86        49        76
  +69       -58       +78       -48       +57       -37
  ____      ____      ____      ____      ____      ____


   98        76        66        48        29        98
  -79       +94       -59       +56       +78       -39
  ____      ____      ____      ____      ____      ____


   88        78        36        94        83        74
  -29       +29       +68       -87       +87       -55
  ____      ____      ____      ____      ____      ____
```

18	9	17	9		15	17
−9	+9	−8	+8		−9	−9

8	7	15	14	8	16	9	14
+6	+7	−7	−8	+9	−7	+9	−5

9	16	16	15	9	6	15	17
+7	−8	−9	−6	+6	+8	−8	−9

16	16	9	7	18	14	14	7
−8	−9	+5	+8	−9	−7	−6	+9

18	14	6		18	17	8
−9	−9	+9		−9	−9	+8

17	5	7	17	18	8	14	18
−8	+9	+9	−9	−9	+7	−9	−9

135

```
   97      189       28                          58
  +90      -96      +49                         +38
 _____    _____    _____                       _____


  169      159       28      179       76       189
  -77      -83      +36      -96      +80       -95
 _____    _____    _____    _____    _____     _____


   95      164       67       39      187        92
  +74      -84      +29      +38      -94       +95
 _____    _____    _____    _____    _____     _____


  178      157      188       26      149        66
  -95      -94      -97      +39      -77       +83
 _____    _____    _____    _____    _____     _____


  146       35                                 168       159
  -63      +29                                 -92       -67
 _____    _____                               _____     _____


   91      157       39      149      149       155
  +58      -85      +26      -58      -86       -72
 _____    _____    _____    _____    _____     _____
```

170

18 drops of honey drip on Joy's bun. She eats nine drops. How many drops are left on her bun?

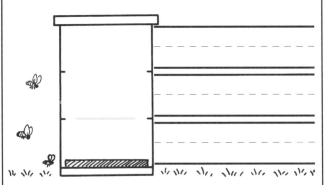

78 bees buzz out of a hive. 67 bees follow them. How many bees is that altogether?

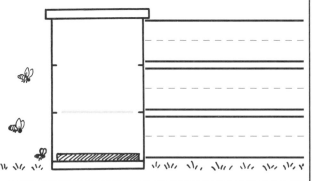

2 cups = 1 pint

2 pints = 1 quart

4 quarts = 1 gallon

Speed
Drill

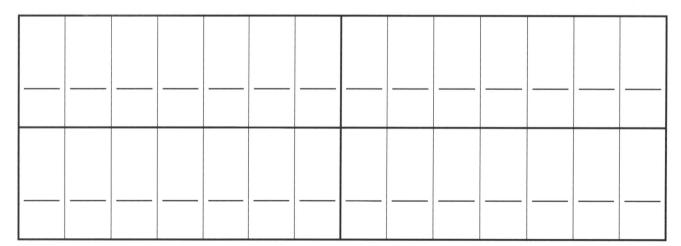

9	17	17	16	9	16
+7	-9	-8	-9	+9	-7

18	8	16	15	9	17
-9	+9	-7	-6	+8	-8

8	6	14	9	16	18	17	7
+9	+9	-5	+9	-9	-9	-9	+9

2	2	3	5	3	7	4	6
4	7	4	4	6	2	5	3
+9	+8	+9	+9	+9	+7	+8	+9

"Whatsoever thy hand findeth to do, do it with thy might." Ecclesiastes 9:10